F*CK THE RULES:

UNLEASH YOUR UNRELENTING DETERMINATION TO LIVE WELL, UNLOCK YOUR POTENTIAL, AND BE HAPPY ON YOUR OWN TERMS

KELLY LYNCH LCSW

ISBN13 Paperback: 978-1-915771-50-6

CONTENTS

To my mom

the strongest, bravest, and most resilient woman I've ever known.

To my dad

my hero for always standing shoulder to shoulder with me.

And to my daughter

You are, and will always be, my favorite person. Being your mom is my greatest joy, my biggest challenge, and the legacy I leave in this world. You inspire me constantly, and I couldn't imagine life any other way than with you in it, being my sidekick as we adventure together. I love you more than coffee. (And I love coffee ***a lot****.)*

DISCLAIMER

The pages of this book are written honestly, in a raw way, and in my most authentic voice. I will speak to you in this book the way I speak in real life – and I believe (when used properly and appropriately) swear words are adjectives and sentence enhancers. While it isn't every other word, they're in there. I also have chosen to throw caution to the wind and intentionally make very obvious grammatical and spelling errors for the sake of euphemism, emphasis, and punny catch phrases, because... levity, friends. It's necessary.

This book is not a memoir; however, I do use stories from my personal life and career throughout the pages I've written. This includes moments from my career in Emergency Medical Services and real calls I've responded to, experiencing a marriage I perceived as frightening and threatening, running multiple businesses while being a single mother, and more. Because this book is not a memoir, the stories told in each chapter do not run in chronological order of how they occurred over the course of my life and careers. Rather, they have been chosen based on relevance to the lessons presented in each chapter. All identifying information of former patients, clients, and colleagues has been removed. In addition, to protect confidentiality, any references to clients and/or patients are amalgamations of many different people in combination with fictitious events, timelines, and characters I've created.

The opinions expressed and the anecdotes recited in this book are based solely on my own perceptions and experiences and should not be construed as facts.

This book is not to be used as a substitute for clinical mental health therapy, medical advice, diagnosis, or treatment. This is intended to be a tool in your personal journey of growth, and the information in this book is for educational and informational purposes only. I will not provide you with a mental health diagnosis at any point in this book, and your use of this book should not be a replacement for receiving any sort of medical or mental health services or interventions. Your use of this book does not create a therapist-client or coach-client relationship between us, and it is not intended to replace the services of a trained mental health professional or medical provider. If you're on the mental health struggle bus, please seek the support of a trained professional. *You deserve it.*

A NOTE ON BREAKING THE RULES

Throughout this book, we are going to look directly at the idea and impact of 'playing by someone else's rules.' Addressing the concept of rules is an incredibly nuanced conversation, and it is impossible to capture every nuance of it in a single book. That said – the concept of breaking rules in order to live meaningful and purposeful lives has existed for many millennia. This is about engaging in the world in a deeper, more authentic way by understanding yourself and your relationship with the world around you as holistically as possible. While the language can be presented differently in different places, this concept can be found woven throughout anti-racism training, the work surrounding efforts to tear apart oppressive systems, various recovery models, and more.

This book addresses the idea of breaking the rules from my own perspective, based on my personal and professional experiences. With that said, please remember that it's always ok to take what you need and freely leave the rest. This isn't about 'one-size-fits-all,' because every single one of us is presented with a different set of life circumstances. We will all use these ideas in different ways, to make those ideas work for us as individuals. And that's the point.

INTRODUCTION

> 'Maybe the journey isn't so much about becoming anything. Maybe it's unbecoming everything that isn't you so you can be who you were meant to be in the first place.'
>
> — PAULO COELHO

What price are you willing to pay to become not only who you've always been meant to be, but to live a happy, whole life, on terms determined solely by you? (That part about living your way – that sounds *good*, doesn't it?)

We get playbooks shoved in our faces constantly throughout life – playbooks that are packed with rules, written by parents / partners / friends / coworkers / kids / hell, even our pets.

When we spend so much time living according to everyone and everything else's rules, it's no wonder any of us can wake up one day, wondering why we feel so shitty. Doing life according to other people's rules will only ever leave us feeling:

Tired
Stressed
Anxious
Overwhelmed
Insecure
And more.

It's a recipe for burnout, for imposter syndrome, for feeling like we're never going to be good enough... You get the point.

Why on earth would we live the life other people are telling us to live if we dream of something completely different, and we dream of a completely different outcome than what they've designed for us?

Remember: their design, their playbooks... it's all made for their comfort and their convenience, and if we play by their rules, we're nothing more than a means to an end. *Screw that.* We (you, me, all of us) are so much more than that, and we all deserve so much more than just existing on behalf of someone else.

Here's where I'm going to shift, though, and move from talking about all of us to talking directly to *you*. You, exactly as you are, are magic. You're a whole entire living, breathing, magical being, made to live an exciting, creative, autonomous life. So, what if I told you that saying 'to hell with it' to their playbooks, tossing those suckers out the window, and starting to write your own rules, is actually the true way to happiness?

I always say to my daughter that I won't ever make her a promise I can't keep, and I'll do the same for you. Taking the steps to lose the weight of the rules other people told you to play by is absolutely the way to happiness, but it doesn't come without a cost, and a bit of pain.

Alex Hormozi said:

> "We pay in time and pain for the person we want to become."

He's right, but here's the thing: if you end up in a cycle of constantly seeking comfort as a way of avoiding pain, you're going to miss the lessons pain is trying to teach you. Pain isn't a good time, obviously, and no one actively chooses to be in pain, which is why it's so easy to get caught up in these weird, useless cycles of trying to avoid it. But the constant avoiding is exactly the thing that:

1. wastes time.
2. leaves you in more pain.

Let's revisit that in a minute while you think about this question:

Who are you?

I'll give you a hint – it's not the things you do for others or the roles you play. Sure, those things matter and they can be key defining parts of what your life looks like, but they're not ever going to be who you are. The roles you play and the things you do are just that – things you do.

So, who are you then?

It's a difficult/not-so-difficult question to answer. It's difficult, because it's not something anyone is really taught how to answer, nor are you given a whole lot of space to look at it very often, all while you're busy getting buried under several metric tons of expectations, 'shoulds', 'have-tos' to fulfill, things you're told to believe in, decisions that have to be made, and more. The list feels endless, right?

In the middle of trying to check all the boxes on this endless to-do list the world hands you, it's wildly simple to lose touch with your core – your truest, most honest self – and slap a set of blinders on to what really matters, while you get busy living as a means-to-an-end for everyone and everything else. This causes people a world of pain, and it's no wonder we have an epidemic of tired, depressed, burnt-out, stressed-out, struggling people, searching for a solution and an end to that pain. But pain is also important.

I firmly believe that pain does one of two things to people, and it depends entirely on how you view the quality and experience of your pain:

1. It shrinks you
2. It expands you.

Ever thought about it that way?

Pain *wants* to be all-consuming, and believe me, it will be if you let it. It's a living, breathing thing that wants to stretch out, expand, and fill in the cracks and crevices in your life that are created by traumatic, sad, overwhelming, scary, and maddening moments. For many people, that's exactly what happens. Every single time you allow pain to do this, it will stop you dead in your tracks, eating up the space that's meant for you to take up, wiping your memory of any recollection of how to solve problems, and halting all progress on you being able to get closer to your dreams.

If you want to get out of pain, you have to stop avoiding, start addressing, and learn from it, once and for all. That's the thing about pain: it's an absolutely *incredible* teacher, and it will continue existing until you're ready to listen to it. In the process of pain showing you that there are spaces to repair and improve on, it's teaching you to *pay attention*. Your job is to make sure you're paying attention to the right thing.

"People change when the amount of pain they're in outweighs their desire to remain the same."

— UNKNOWN

Once you learn the lessons it's trying to teach, that's when pain starts to transform into triumph, you start to mature, the season you're in begins to shift, and you start changing into the person you were always meant to be. That's the moment pain stops shrinking you and begins expanding you.

Listen, living according to your own rules doesn't mean you won't ever experience pain again. It doesn't mean you won't ever experience a traumatic *something* or be set magically free from having some sort of chaos you have to deal with from time to time. It doesn't mean that hurtful or harmful circumstances won't ever happen again. These are all part of the inevitabilities of life. If anyone ever tries to sell you on having a perfect life, without facing another problem ever again, and you buy it, I've got a bridge I can sell you, too.

Life isn't perfect, and it's not meant to be. It's meant to be learned from, experienced, enjoyed, cared for, protected – all the things. *Living well doesn't mean living perfectly.* It means living on your terms, your way, for your own reasons. When you get so caught up in the playbooks thrown at you, it's easy to get caught up in feeling like you're doing it all wrong if you don't live the way you're told to. But the price you pay in doing that is the price of losing yourself to the expectations of others. And that's why answering the question of 'who are you' can feel so incredibly difficult. To lose the difficulty of that question and step into the ease of it instead is a matter of slowing down, learning, growing, and doing you, your way.

Now, living on your terms, according to the rules you write for yourself, also comes at a cost – it may mean that people leave your life, that you have to move on from certain places, and that you'll have outgrown certain seasons you're in right now. Your job is to decide if paying that price is worth it.

If you keep people, places, and things hanging around because you're not ready to let go, you're scared, you're seeking out comfort, or anything else, you're inviting the opportunity for those things to interrupt your process of becoming.

One day, as I was wasting time on TikTok (as one does when one is avoiding doing paperwork), I scrolled by a video by Felecia Hatcher in the process of giving a speech. She talked about how she had been impacted while listening to two women talk to each other. She tells the story of one woman asking the other:

 *'Who are you, uninterrupted?'*

She goes on in this video to explain the importance of asking yourself what your life would look like if nothing stood in the way.

Pain is a thing that desperately wants to interrupt us, first and foremost. If you allow it to do what it wants to do in that aspect, it's going to shrink you – every single time – because your brain will want to shut it down out of a desire for safety.

However, when you slow down enough to examine the interruption, ask it questions, and *learn* from it, you get to step into a position of control. Of power. Of magnitude. Of becoming.

Leadership [lēdərˌShip] *noun:* the action of leading a group of people or an organization

The process of undoing everything that you were told to be, in order to become who you were always meant to be, while writing your own playbook and living by your own set of rules, is the art of practicing self-leadership. And becoming your own best leader is really what this book is all about.

Unearthing the most authentic version of you from under the crap the world piled on top of you – the trauma, responsibility, pressure to perform, fit the 'mold', and more – requires you to step into a self-leadership role in your life. If leadership is all about action and directing a group of people towards a goal, then self-leadership is about internalizing the action and practicing self-direction instead. The act of practicing self-leadership means you've decided that pain is no longer allowed to interrupt you or interfere with your ability to become your truest self and live life your own way. It's ok to feel the pain – quite simply, that's just you being human. You're going to feel it, whether you want to or not. In the process of feeling, though, remembering that you are capable of doing hard things, you are capable of persevering, and making it through with the right supports and skills – that right there is you being unwilling to let pain interrupt you. And that's badass.

In 2022, I was working with a client who was constantly struggling because of overthinking, making things harder than they needed to be because of poor choices... You get the idea. Hard, emotionally taxing, hurtful things kept happening in their life, and they were stuck – bigtime. They had been a client for several years at that point, but I had never seen them as stuck as they were that year. I wanted so badly to support them and offer them a different way of looking at things, so that they could start to regain some traction and build momentum again on working through the problems they were dealing with. I was turning the issues they faced over and over in my head, until I started realizing that there was a sequence to the things we had worked on over the years, and that this particular sequence worked really, really well for them. They just needed a name for it. As I considered that sequence, I was honestly dumbfounded when it dawned on me that this was a sequence I had been taking all my clients through throughout my career – but it was also how I lived my life. It was the moment GRIIT and POWER were born.

GRIIT, a system of mindset and self-leadership development, keeps you looking forward to what's next, while helping you identify, learn, and truly understand your 'most important' lessons. POWER is a system designed specifically for managing and/or resolving the problems none of us can plan for or predict, and it keeps you from getting stuck in life's quicksand. They matter equally for different reasons, and they go hand in hand.

<u>GRITT</u>

Growth

Resilience

Identity

Integrity

Training

POWER

Pause for Perspective
Observe and Organize
Work the Problem
Express the Impact
Recover

In the process of engaging with and building your self-leadership ability in order to live well, it's important to have both proactive and reactive strategies you can pull from. GRIIT is proactive, because it keeps you looking ahead, while POWER is reactive, because it helps you figure out how to navigate the problems that naturally happen in the process of living.

Think about it this way – it's a bit like riding a bicycle. In order to stay upright, you have to look ahead at where you're going. By looking forward, you're keeping your center of gravity lined up so that you can balance properly. The better your balance, the harder your legs can push to propel you forward, and the further you'll go. That's what GRIIT does for you, because it supports your mindset, reminding you what matters most while keeping in perspective what you're capable of doing and accomplishing.

But, what happens if you look down while riding your bicycle? Your center of gravity is all of a sudden thrown off, and you fall over. Or what if you hit an obstacle in the road that you couldn't see coming because it's so small, like a nail or a small stone, and you get a flat tire? You have to figure out how to get back up again after falling, repair or replace your flat tire, and keep an eye out for any more obstacles or distractions. This is what

POWER does for you. By helping you figure out strategies for addressing the problems you can't plan for or predict, it helps you get back up after you've fallen or gotten stuck, so that you can get right back on track with living well.

Throughout this book, you will learn the details of these two methods, why they matter, and how you can apply them in your life. I'll tell you stories from my life and how I've used them to survive some really dark moments, while telling you other stories about how I and many of my clients have used these methods to go and thrive. I'll walk you through exercises in certain parts, and give you different options and ways to apply the ideas inside each method. And that's the most beautiful part about these methods – *they're not rules*. They're strategies and ideas, and you get to decide how you want to use them as you write your very own playbook.

Each chapter will close with a journal prompt, for you to begin the process of meeting yourself and exploring what your version of self-leadership and problem-solving will look like.

People go to self-help books in search of answers – we want to know 'why, what, and how.'

Why do I feel the way I do/Why am I stuck?

What is it that I don't know?

How can I learn what I don't know, and how do I apply it?

How do I fix it, if it's crappy/How do I enhance it, if it's great?

Most self-help books will give you some sort of answer for the 'what and why' parts, but many do not answer the 'how.' That's not how we roll here. You're going to get an answer (and a deep, detailed one at that) to all three parts, but then you have to be ready, willing, and able to do the work. Having the answer to the question is just the first step: the next steps are to take the time to make sure you're putting those answers to work for you.

Because when you do, the reward is what you're left with...

A greater sense of self, a more fulfilling life, a deeper sense of joy... You get the idea.

The most controversial, rebellious, audacious, and awe-inspiring thing you could ever possibly do is to live life fully on your terms, your way, and according to your own rules.

Audacity [aw-das-i-tee] *noun:* intrepid boldness; bold or arrogant disregard of normal restraints

The word 'audacity' has taken on a very particular (and not so awesome) meaning in present day society. I ask that you take a moment and just hang out with this word and its definition. When you decide to toss the playbooks that got dropped in your lap and write your own, living by your own rules, that requires you to be audacious. It's been said many times that the ultimate rebellion is personal success, and I'm honestly not sure I could think of a better example of the positive, healthy side of audacity.

I want you to use this book, these ideas, and these strategies and skills to achieve a level of success, happiness, and a fucking badass life that is so incredibly rad it far exceeds the comfort level of the people you're currently choosing to surround yourself with. I challenge you to expand, over and over and over again, beyond the point you have ever imagined possible.

Be rebellious and live with the audacity of someone with unrelenting determination to succeed.

Your most enduring legacy will always be the one of you standing up for yourself, choosing yourself – over and over again – and doing it all your way, on your terms, and in your own time.

This is your manual for learning how to lead yourself and live boldly, once and for all.

Let's get started.

PART I

GRIIT

'To become and unbecome lies in your hand, your willpower defines how far.'

— MOFOLUKE AYOOLA

We're inundated constantly with messages and 'rules' – in the news, TV, movies, ads, radio shows, fashion, in the ways we're raised and in the things we're told to believe... literally everywhere – about what we're supposed to become; what we're supposed to do with our lives or strive towards achieving; how much money we're supposed to make; the way we're supposed to speak; what size jeans we're supposed to be able to squeeze into in order to be deemed attractive; what kind of education we're supposed to want and get; and more.

It's overwhelming.

No wonder it's so easy to get completely lost in it all, trying to constantly do and be the 'right' thing, thinking that by doing what's expected of you or what you're told you're supposed to believe, you'll get to become a good person and be exactly who you're meant to be.

Eventually, this just turns into you becoming who other people wanted you to be, instead of you being who you were meant to be.

The process of becoming who you were always meant to be, as Paulo Coehlo put it, has to begin with figuring out how to courageously say 'fuck the rules' you've been told to live according to, in order to discover your truest self and figure out how to live on your own terms. Just remember – the 'fuck it' you toss out to the world is based on context, situation, and circumstance. Not all people are going to have the same access, ability, perspective, or mindset as you do, and it's important to give some grace to that. And then going back to doing you, your way.

That's what GRIIT is all about. In order to learn how to become who you were always meant to be, so you can be happy and live the way you truly want, you have to learn what got you 'here' in the first place. When you work on quieting the 'white noise' of the world around you, and you stop trying to live up to everyone else's expectations of who they want or need you to be... all of a sudden you have the space to start figuring out how to live life on your terms, your way.

GRIIT stands for:

Growth
Resilience
Identity
Integrity
Training

Each pillar is a guide to not only understanding what things can happen that get in your way and how to recognize them, but also how to work through – and eventually beyond – those pitfalls. Once you're able to recognize where potential barriers can pop up and how you're affected by them, that's when you can really put GRIIT into action and do life in whatever way tickles your fancy the most.

To put each pillar to work for you, you'll have to go back to parts of your past and re-evaluate, in order to look for lessons and gold nuggets that you need to gather up so you can move forward productively. It's important, in the process of looking at past experiences, that you make sure to only visit – don't unpack and stay there. If you unpack, settle in, and snuggle up with the past, the cycle of living on everyone else's terms will simply start all over. Observe the past in order to leverage it – *don't be its cuddle buddy.*

As you use GRIIT to unbecome, and then become, remember this:

This is about being proactive *always*, so you may live boldly, live well, and live on your terms. Not anyone else's.

This is where you get to do 'it' your way - no matter what the 'it' is.

And here we go!

1

GROWTH

'Becoming is better than being.'

— CAROL DWECK, *MINDSET: THE NEW PSYCHOLOGY OF SUCCESS*

Changing your life begins with building a growth mindset, and to build a growth mindset, we must start with understanding what a growth mindset is and what gets in its way.

It was somewhere around 2013 when I first heard the terms 'fixed mindset' and 'growth mindset'. I was working for a community mental health agency and heard two of my coworkers use these terms in conversation with each other. I had never heard these terms prior to that moment, so I asked what they meant, and as each term was explained to me, I remember feeling the white-hot flame of embarrassment creep up my neck, into my cheeks, coming to rest at the tops of my ears, making them feel like they'd burst into flames any second.

I'd been working as a social worker for four years, I was fully licensed for independent practice, and, by all appearances, I was a halfway decent therapist. But under the surface, I was constantly questioning myself, my knowledge, my skill sets, and the choices I made in how I guided my clients.

Hearing these terms – fixed mindset and growth mindset – left me feeling so small and insecure because I was sure this was something I should have learned in graduate school. I was struggling with realizing how much I still had to learn, despite having four years of experience, and I felt trapped by feelings of inadequacy. Without really, truly realizing it, I had taken a headfirst dive into the deep end of the imposter syndrome pool, and was just waiting for someone to catch on and tell everyone what a fraud of a therapist I was. In other words, my mindset sucked.

Sound familiar?

If it does, fear not, friend. This is *normal.*

GRIIT begins with Growth, because everything about the other pillars extends from a growth mindset. If you're going to go and live your best life, you've got to have the right foundation, and that starts with the right mindset.

Let's define what fixed and growth mindsets really are.

Carol Dweck is the researcher who coined these terms through her research on mindset in school-age children. Throughout her early career, she notes in her book 'Mindset: The New

Psychology of Success' that she was obsessed with trying to figure out how people cope with the experience of failure. Conducting experiments in which she had school-age children work on progressively harder puzzles, she discovered that they either resigned themselves to failure once they saw the puzzles getting harder, or they got excited the more challenging the puzzles became. Through the process of these and other experiments, she realized how different people really are, and how many of these differences are a conversation of *both* nature *and* nurture.

She defines a fixed mindset as:

> 'Believing that your qualities are carved in stone – the *fixed* mindset – creates an urgency to prove yourself over and over.'

On the other hand, she defines a growth mindset as:

> 'This *growth* mindset is based on the belief that your basic qualities are things you can cultivate through your efforts, your strategies, and help from others. Although people may differ in every which way, everyone can change and grow through application and experience.'

If we make that even simpler, a fixed mindset is the period at the end of a sentence. It's very final. On the other hand, a growth mindset is the comma in the middle of a sentence, encouraging it to continue.

So how does mindset develop?

Let's go back to what Carol Dweck realized about the differences in people. She realized it was about *both* nature *and* nurture, and how they influenced and worked with each other. Until that point, many researchers and scholars had argued that human behavior was a result of *either* all nature *or* all nurture. Simply put, our friend Carol realized how the idea of 'both/and' mattered so much more than the idea of 'either/or.' She realized she had to emphasize the *dialectics* of mindset.

In psychology, the concept of dialectics is actually very important. It's a reminder that more than one opposite thing can be true at the same time, and that one thing does not cancel out or minimize the other. They're simply two opposite things that managed to co-exist. An example of this could be feeling in a moment of struggle that you're doing the best you can, while also knowing at the same time that you want to do better. Both are true; - you're doing the best you can in the process of struggling, *and* you know that you want to do better than that.

When we think about the differences between a fixed and growth mindset, a fixed mindset is very black and white. It is the purest representation of 'either/or' because it's 'I'm either a success, or I'm a failure'. There is no option between; there's no alternative. On the other hand, a growth mindset is grey because it leaves room for more. It's the 'both/and' in that it leaves room for things like 'I'm failing right now, so what do I need to learn or do differently so I can get a better outcome?'

Notice how I wrote that out, too. A fixed mindset is typically a representation of who someone believes they actually are, versus a growth mindset usually being a representation of how someone views their skill sets and behaviors. Big, huge, mighty difference.

I'll never forget the day Dan stomped into my office for the first time.

I'd known him for years. The first time I met him, I was a young, new Emergency Medical Technician (EMT) and he was an instructor in one of my classes. I didn't see him for several years after that class ended, but came upon him again when I had gotten a new job with a different EMS company and he was working for one of the neighboring fire departments as a firefighter/paramedic. We were always friendly with each other, and stayed in touch on social media when I became a therapist and stopped working on the ambulance.

He gruffed at me that first day as he practically fell onto my couch. 'Kelly, if you treat me like a project, I'm never coming back.' I remember staring at him with (what felt like) wide eyes, hoping he wouldn't notice the nervous gulp I took when he said that, and responded with simply 'Ok'.

Dan had gone to therapy before, and let's just say it wasn't good. Very early on in our relationship, I learned that other therapists had left Dan feeling like a pet project, as if he was some broken toy they were tasked with repairing. He sought me out with the hope that I would understand his thoughts, feelings, and opinions better than his previous therapists since we had similar life experiences of working in emergency services.

Over the course of the first few months of working together, Dan revealed just how much he was struggling. His home life was falling apart – he was disconnected from his kids, he and his wife were constantly arguing, his finances weren't in great shape, and the stress of it all was starting to trickle over into work... and people were noticing. He was worried about his reputation and didn't want people to worry about him. But over time he also admitted how exhausted he was from feeling like he had to take care of everyone all the time, and wasn't able to allow other people to take care of him. He struggled, feeling like he was expected to always be strong, and hated feeling judged or labeled as an asshole when his stress got the better of him.

Dan was struggling with cognitive dissonance and confirmation bias; we've all got a bit of Dan within us.

Cognitive dissonance refers to the uncomfortable feeling of experiencing two or more thoughts that contradict each other. We want to 'make it make sense', which leaves us feeling like one thought has to be more true or correct than the other thought. This creates friction and frustration in our thought process, because there's pressure to need to choose the 'best' thought.

On the flip side, confirmation bias is the process of seeking out information that confirms what we want to be true. If you believe the Boston Red Sox are the best baseball team, you're not going to go and ask a Yankees fan who the best team is. You're going to ask another Red Sox fan, because they'll give you the answer that confirms what you're already thinking and feeling.

Dan's cognitive dissonance showed up in his belief that he had to be strong all the time, but also how he was deeply exhausted from the stress and pressure he was under at home. He had a hell of a lot of confirmation bias surrounding his belief that he basically had to be everyone's hero, but he was also totally pissed about it because it left him feeling completely unseen as a person. He believed he was a means to an end for other people, and that he wasn't able to stop being that because it was a role he chose. He was completely torn between what it meant to him to continue being that hero persona, versus being vulnerable with the people he loved and letting them know how much he was struggling. Dan truly believed he couldn't continue to be a hero while also being a vulnerable human; it had to be one or the other.

Dan had an incredibly positive reputation in his department and his community as a talented, experienced firefighter/paramedic. He was respected by his coworkers and the department chief, and was held in high regard by other emergency services in surrounding towns. He had won service awards, was a paramedic and firefighting instructor, and had multiple decades of service under his belt. His friends viewed him as a good, reliable, strong man, and the wives and girlfriends of his coworkers regularly made comments to his wife about how lucky she was to be married to Dan. There were piles upon piles of confirmation that Dan *was* the quintessential hero, and with a career spanning several decades at that point, it had become his whole personality.

Between the cognitive dissonance surrounding how exhausted he was as a person and the way he was experiencing his confirmation bias surrounding having to be 'the hero', Dan was completely stuck in a fixed mindset. He knew he wanted out, feeling the way he did, but wasn't able to see the way out on his own.

Take a moment here to think about your inner Dan.

Can you relate to his story? How so?

Think about where cognitive dissonance and confirmation bias show up in your life. What do they each affect in your life? How do they affect your view on those things? How do they impact the way you view yourself?

This is the hard work that, a lot of the time, people don't really want to do because it requires that we look in the mirror. Getting comfortable with self-reflection is a pretty uncomfortable process, if we're being totally honest. It means challenging and confronting the things we've been told and taught throughout our lives, and how those things have shaped the way we view both ourselves and the world around us. It means looking at what we believe, and asking if those are ideas we want to continue to believe in.

So why does self-reflection matter so much?

Well, this is the process of metacognition. Without getting too existential or going down an Alice in Wonderland type of rabbit hole, the basic idea of metacognition, sometimes described as 'thinking about your thinking', means taking a step back and zooming out on a situation and what you're doing so you can figure out what's working and what isn't.

Each time we actively engage in metacognition and self-reflection, we're taking a step *away* from a fixed mindset and moving a step *towards* a growth mindset, because we're giving ourselves the opportunity to reflect and learn something.

There are three steps to the cycle of metacognition:

1. Self-monitoring: observing what you're doing.
2. Self-evaluating: making a judgment call on how you're doing with something you've been trying or a skill you've been using.
3. Self-regulating: examining what's working and what's not, so you can make changes and improvements.

The more regularly we walk through this cycle of 'check in / evaluate / adjust', the more apt we are to get – and stay – in a growth mindset because we're constantly looking for ways to improve, grow, and evolve.

But what if bad shit keeps happening in your life?

Well, there's another spicy little bias that's important to know about, and if you let it, it will wreak absolute havoc on your mindset. Introducing...

Negativity bias!

It's easy to get 'lost in the weeds' with an idea like this, so let's keep it simple. Negativity bias is the idea that humans are much more impacted by negative events than positive ones, to the point that negativity often significantly influences and shapes our thoughts, feelings, and behaviors, and can have some super-duper-extra unsavory effect on our psychological state.

This bias is so ingrained into the behavioral patterns of human beings that there really isn't an 'un-wiring' it, and it actually is something that has been extremely important throughout time. Think about it this way: once upon a time, there were dinosaurs roaming the earth. You, as the wonderful cave person that you were, wandered out of your cave one day to go hunt and forage for yourself and your family. All of a sudden, BAM! There's a dinosaur that was hiding behind a boulder, hunting you, and now you've got to beat feet to safety just as fast as possible. The next time you head out to hunt and forage, you either avoid that same area entirely and choose a different hunting and foraging spot, or you go back to the same spot but you're *way* more careful. The choice to pick a new spot or approach the same spot with extreme caution is based on the fact that you now associate it with something negative: *fear of harm*.

Negativity bias through the millennia has shown up in the context of literally keeping us alive, thus becoming a really important part of our survival instincts. But we don't need it today the same way we needed it when dinosaurs lurked around every corner. And yet this spicy bias hangs around.

So what does this have to do with mindset?

Everything, friend. *Everything*.

When you focus on the people, places, things, and ideas around you that have left you feeling stuck, insecure, overwhelmed, scared, doubting yourself (hello, imposter syndrome!), and more, it's because something has happened that triggered your negativity bias to kick into high gear.

Once that happens, here comes your cognitive dissonance, confirmation bias, and that 'either/or' perspective, all of which will land you square in the middle of a fixed mindset.

Simply put, negativity bias becomes a gateway for all those other sneaky little things to enter, getting you to question your every step, because it's trying to protect you. But in today's day and age, instead of negativity bias keeping you safe when you're trying something new or working on bettering yourself, it's only going to keep you small. It doesn't want you to try that 'new thing' because that new thing feels unpredictable. It's going to tell you 100% of the time that you shouldn't do it, you shouldn't ever change, and you shouldn't ever risk anything.

Remember our friend Dan?

Dan was fighting with himself over change. He knew he was miserable staying the way he was; his perspectives and beliefs weren't working for him anymore. But to create change, he had to challenge everything he had ever known and believed in. That was a major threat to the hero part of his personality, so his negativity bias kicked in to try to protect him from himself. That's when his arguments with himself started, knowing that he needed to change and needed things in his environments to change, while wanting, at the same time, for everything to remain the same.

If you know your inner Dan is alive and well – trying to resist change at every possible opportunity yet also resenting the way things are – let's start shifting that.

At the start of this chapter, we began with talking about the differences between a growth mindset and a fixed mindset, along with what challenges pop up in the process of building a growth mindset.

Now it's time to get busy working on behaviors to shift your mindset.

These behaviors are largely self-explanatory. The trick, my friend, is in the application and the practice.

This list is not exhaustive of all the things you can do to begin working on shifting your mindset, but it's a really damn good place to start:

1. **Pay attention to the way you speak to yourself, about yourself.** We all can get caught up in being our own worst critics, but when you're working on shifting your mindset, it's important to make sure your personal critiques also include a bit of kindness. The more positive and non-judgmental you are to yourself, the more apt you'll be (over time – this isn't instant!) to behave with more self-respect, really paying attention to maintaining your values and ethical beliefs, and ultimately shifting what you believe you're capable of accomplishing.
2. **Stop seeking everyone else's approval and remind yourself that you're already your own best expert.** When you're constantly seeking approval from the people you're surrounded by, you stop trusting

yourself, your instincts, and your strengths/talents. Each time you lean more into your instincts, you give yourself more opportunity to poke around and explore what you're naturally good at, along with having more chance at improving upon your weaknesses. Spend some time getting to know those parts of you – you'll end up cultivating more authenticity that way, too.

3. **Learn to enjoy the journey.** Savoring is a whole thing, friend. Look it up. When we take time to savor the process of becoming, it's amazing what happens. The destination doesn't stop mattering, but it does matter a hell of a lot less. You realize over time that it's way more exciting to learn from people who've come before you, you start being more realistic about the amount of time it takes to learn new things so that you can change and level up in life, and so much more. The lessons gathered along the way start to become the reward, and you realize it's not the pace of change that matters, but rather the effort put into creating that change.
4. **Embrace the reward of taking calculated risks – even when they fail.** We're going to talk a lot more about risk and risk-taking in the next chapter, but for now, focus on this. You're not going to learn, grow, and change without taking at least some degree of risk a whole bunch of times. Sometimes, the risk you take is going to pay off big time and you'll get the outcome you wanted. And then other times, it's going to fail and you'll be left feeling like your efforts were as much of a dud as your last date with the old high school quarterback (or cheerleading captain, for that matter)

> who's still living out the glory days and never actually grew up. *Giant* flop. Here's the thing: you can learn from both outcomes. Every single time you take a risk and attempt something new, you have the opportunity to gather information about what works, and what doesn't. The more information you have at your disposal, the more opportunity you have to 'hone your craft' – fine-tuning the way you show up to different parts of your life- and level the fuck up. The risk, no matter the outcome, is worth it, because of the information and the lessons it provides.

And as we close with starting to chat about risk, we're now moving into what it means to build resilience.

Onward!

GROWTH JOURNAL PROMPT

In what ways do I allow fear to hold me back from living a more expansive life? What am I ready, willing, and able to start doing differently right now to work on building a growth mindset?

2

RESILIENCE

'Most of the time you don't need more information, you need more courage.'

— JAMES CLEAR

I was out to lunch one day with a close friend, and was telling her about a recent instructor certification class I had taken. I signed up for this class because not only was I extremely interested in the subject matter, but I wanted to push myself to see how far I could go and how much I could handle with that particular topic. But the topic of the class also hailed from a male-dominated field, and I was the only woman who had signed up.

I'll never forget sitting in the parking lot outside the building the class was being held in. I watched each man walk in who had also signed up – large, hulking figures being carried with the confidence of knowing they belonged, simply by rights of what they had between their legs. As I sat in my car watching them file in, I thought to myself, 'What the fuck are you doing, Kell? You don't belong here; you're going to fail. Just drive away now, and no one has to know this ever even happened.'

But see - someone *would* know. *I* would know. And I couldn't live with knowing I had given up on something that was important to me and had let fear win. So, I went in.

I'd taken classes in the past for this particular topic and had loved them all, but I had never been the sole female in the room. When I walked in the classroom, the reaction was a mix of some men who were so unbothered by my presence that they didn't skip a beat from what they were doing (to my absolute relief), others who looked up and rolled their eyes, while others looked at me in such a way that it felt like they were staring straight through me. It was wildly intimidating, which was probably the point.

I found a seat at the back of the room so that I could hide as much as possible, because my fear of 'what if' had left my heart pounding so loudly I could barely hear myself think. The man to my left said a pleasant 'Hi' and introduced himself, while the one to my right snickered about me to the guy on his other side. For the sake of this story, let's call this fellow 'Snickers'.

I ended up being paired off for exercises with Snickers at the start of the class (go figure), and quickly discovered his initial prick-ish presentation was absolutely valid. He made no secret about his feelings regarding me being in that class and threw in digs wherever he could. That, quite frankly, pissed me off, because I wasn't about to allow him – or anyone else in that room – to make me feel small or like I didn't belong.

As I described the class and my experiences of it to my friend, I explained to her the determination I felt to not ever be small, feel small, or allow someone like Snickers to actually make me small. She and I talked about how that meant I had to have a close relationship with fear and the fear of failure, but then she said something that stopped me in my tracks. She said,

'But Kelly, I view you as being so fearless. I'm really shocked to hear you talk about being scared.'

I remember chuckling a little, explaining to her that I'm scared basically all the time, *but* I'm absolutely unwilling to allow my fear to make my decisions for me. I went on to explain to her how that stubbornness of not giving in to fear helped me stand up for myself to Snickers, how it helped me rescue him in front of the class during a group exercise he was floundering with, and how the instructor for the course told the class to follow in my example of how I dealt with that particular exercise successfully. It was at that moment – when the instructor told the men to watch what I was doing – that I won their respect, and the respect of Snickers.

Snickers went on to thank me for my help during that exercise, and he chilled out. He even stepped in to help me when I was struggling with a different exercise, and at the end of the class, we shook hands and wished each other good luck. Once he realized I was a friend and not a foe, Snickers was pretty alright.

And, oh yeah... I passed the class.

Take a second here and think about the last scary thing you did. What was it? Aside from being scary, what else did you feel in the process of doing that thing? What made you choose to do it? Did you get the result you wanted, or did you achieve your goal? If you didn't, what did you learn from that experience? Would you be willing to do it again?

Experiences like these are where we're tested and, in many ways, they can be the proving grounds for all of us to really learn and discover not only what we're made of, but how much we're actually capable of. And that, that's where we begin with resilience.

Resilience is defined as:

> 'the capacity to withstand or recover quickly from difficulties; toughness'.

A quick Google search on 'how to build resilience' results in 427,000,000 hits, so I think it's pretty safe to say that people both want to know how to build resilience, and also really struggle with it. In order to build it up, it's important to understand that resilience is a skill that requires a growth mindset first and foremost. This is why GRIIT is what it is – everything builds off the previous pillars.

Dr. Kenneth Ginsberg is a pediatrician specializing in Adolescent Medicine at the Children's Hospital of Pennsylvania. In his research on resilience in children and adolescents, he found there are seven pillars of building and supporting resilience in youth, which he calls the '7 Cs'. Much of his work is based off the research on resilience from the Positive Youth Development Movement, along with the work of Rick Little at the International Youth Foundation.

Dr. Ginsberg notes the '7 Cs' are:

1. Competence
2. Confidence
3. Connection
4. Character
5. Contribution
6. Coping
7. Control

I'm going to let you in on a little secret here: just because Dr. Ginsberg's work is centered around resilience in children, this doesn't mean these pillars aren't for you as an adult. In fact, these pillars become even more important as we age and, throughout the remainder of this book, we'll end up touching on all of them in some form or fashion.

That said, I believe the two most important pillars of resilience are the first two, 'Competence' and 'Confidence'. These are what we'll focus on and break down to a microscopic level for the remainder of this chapter. If you want to build resilience, building up your competence and your confidence are the most important areas to focus on, because they are truly the foundation resilience is built on. We're going to skip the other Cs in this chapter, but I pinky promise you that they'll show up in other ways throughout the rest of the book.

Let's start by breaking down and understanding competence.

According to the American Psychological Association's Dictionary of Psychology, competence is: 'the ability to exert control over one's life, to cope with specific problems effectively, and to make changes to one's behavior and one's environment, as opposed to the mere ability to adjust or adapt to circumstances as they are.'

If we translate that from psychobabble into English, competence is simply the ability to do stuff really well.

But how do we get to there?

While you're on the way to building competence, you're going to have to do a lot of things, a lot of times, and probably screw it up a whole bunch. Sounds fun, right? *<Not...>*

But it matters, though. In the process of doing, trying, failing, doing, trying, and failing over and over again, you're actively engaging in the process of building self-efficacy. Self-efficacy, originally coined by psychologist Albert Bandura, is the belief in your ability to do what's needed so you can reach your goals. It affects basically every area of our lives as human beings; it helps us to feel accomplished and is both discovered and built upon by persevering through adversity.

As we feel more and more accomplished, we're going to feel better about ourselves, we'll have a stronger belief that we can recover faster from shitty situations, and we'll feel less overall stress. On the flip side, the less accomplished we feel, the more vulnerable we become to things like anxiety and depression, and the easier it becomes to lose faith in our ability to both handle and recover from challenges.

Go back and read those two sentences again. Did you notice how self-confidence just snuck into the chat?

That's right, friend. Self-efficacy and self-confidence are inextricably linked. The more effective you both believe and feel you are in doing, trying, learning through failure, and recovering from failure, the more confident you become. By choosing actively to risk failure so that you can learn how to be more effective and competent in chasing your goals, the more confident you'll become over time in yourself, your knowledge, and ability to actually achieve your goals.

And yet, choosing actively to risk failure is really fucking scary. Let's shift our focus now to unpack how competence and confidence can be built through risk-taking, thus resulting in greater resilience.

When I chose to walk into that class full of dude bros, I had (mostly) no idea what to expect. I didn't know anyone, I'd never taken an instructor course for literally anything before, and I felt completely in over my head. But I walked in anyway. Why? Because I decided that taking the risk of walking into that class and possibly failing it (and completely embarrassing myself in the process) was a *better* option than not walking in at all.

Talking about risk-taking makes people really uncomfortable. I mean really, really, seriously uncomfortable.

We've built a society around us that praises high achievement and encourages people to consistently work harder and harder in order to achieve more and more.

In the process of that, we've not only stressed and burned each other out by constantly demanding more, but we've also lost sight of the difference between what it means to take calculated risks and what it means to be reckless. Let's get recklessness squared away before we proceed, because – let's face it – you've got to 'check yo'self before you wreck yo'self'.

Being reckless means doing something without taking the time to consider the consequences of whatever that something is. Think about it this way:

When's the last time you just blindly followed orders from your boss? Do you trust their leadership enough that you feel confident in blindly following them?

Or...

When's the last time you were about do something with friends, had a spidey-sense moment of 'maybe this is a bad idea', and then immediately dismissed the feeling with a 'nah, fuck it', throwing caution to the wind and doing it anyway? How'd it work out for you?

Every time you dismiss your intuition, blindly trust or follow someone who has even a teensy bit of power in your life, or act impulsively, you're being reckless. No bueno, friend. Don't do that.

Recklessness is a recipe for destruction, and it's really a matter of time until recklessness catches up with itself and crashes and burns.

Instead of allowing recklessness to run rampant through your life like an unchecked toddler, you need to start understanding the nuances of risk.

First, know that risk is unavoidable. It's just part of life, and you're going to always have a relationship with risk, whether you like it or not. In order to understand how to be more confident in managing risk, there are two groups of ideas to get familiar with:

1. Risk prevention and risk mitigation
2. Risk tolerance and risk aversion

Risk prevention is essentially the things you can do to get ahead of a potential issue. If you go to your local YMCA to swim, take a minute to notice all the signs hanging that remind you (and those unchecked toddler folk) not to run in the bathroom, halls, and near the pool, because it will more than likely be slippery and the nice people at the Y don't want you to fall and sue them. If staff catch you moving and grooving a bit too fast, they're also likely going to ask you to cool it and slow down. The reminder to use caution is risk prevention; the choice to disregard the reminder is recklessness.

Risk mitigation, on the other hand, is about trying to control risks and reduce their impact on certain events. You know, as a driver and car owner, that your vehicle needs specific maintenance at periodic intervals in order to stay in good working order and keep you on the road. In fact, as I'm writing this, my car is due for an oil change. If you and I don't make the time to prioritize the needed maintenance for our cars, they're inevitably going to start having issues. Now if you have a newer car, maybe you can get away for quite some time without doing anything to keep it running nicely. But if your car is anything like how my very first car was (a teal green, '92 Dodge Shadow named 'Stella', a phenomenal jalopy who burned through oil like one of the Real Housewives of *wherever* burning through husbands), you've got to be practically militant about maintenance or that car is going to throw an epic temper tantrum on short notice. Risk mitigation will wax and wane depending on the situation you're applying it to, but it's always something that needs to be taken into account.

Now risk tolerance and risk aversion, on the other hand, are going to directly affect the choices you make in the process of practicing prevention and mitigation. This is a lot of information, and it can get confusing, so take your time here.

Risk tolerance is exactly what it sounds like – it's how much risk you're willing to tolerate in the process of chasing down goals. Having a higher tolerance for risk means you're going to take on more things that might make other people squeamish, and while you may end up failing more often than other people (because, let's face it, not every risk is going to end well), you may end up winning more, too.

On the flip side, risk aversion is all about how much you do to avoid risk. It's those moments when you dig your heels in and refuse to do something unless or until you can mostly predict the outcome, because the 'not knowing' makes you just a little too green around the gills.

Here's the thing: all of us are made up of different combinations of risk tolerance and risk aversion, and there's no wrong answer for what that looks like for you. Whatever your combination is, and however this shows up for you, it's going to be based on the experiences you've had in your life. For example, I'm super-duper risk tolerant with business decisions because I've learned from watching other people and the impact of the choices they've made, and many of the risks I've taken have worked out well. But when it comes to my retirement, saving for it, and figuring out what to invest in so that my retirement funds can grow, I'm *way* risk averse. I lost a lot of money in the stock market crash in 2008, along with losing most of my retirement funds in my divorce (and having to rebuild it... total bummer), so I've been risk averse about investments ever since those two major events.

What matters with risk tolerance and risk aversion is really just understanding what they are and where they show up in your life, because they're both going to color in what you do for risk prevention and mitigation.

So, what will you do when a risk comes knocking at your door?

Will you answer, knowing it *might* be the thing you've been waiting for that will help you reach your dreams? Or will you run away, screaming in fear at the sight of the unknown? While there's a time and a place for letting risk aversion lead the way, risk tolerance is something you're going to have to learn how to stand shoulder to shoulder with if you're working on building a growth mindset.

The moments in which you choose to lean into tolerating risk will be based on your willingness to be both courageous *and* brave.

Most people, most of the time, think of courage and bravery as synonymous. Well, they're not.

<Cue confusion>

In the process of building resilience and being resilient, taking risks, and feeling both effective and confident in what we're doing and why we're doing it, it's important to understand the role that courage and bravery play in making all of those things happen.

I've said for many years now that courage is the feeling or idea we get when we're choosing intentionally to do something risky, despite being afraid, and bravery is the follow-through on that idea. Let's take that a step further, shall we?

If courage is the feeling we experience in the moment of making the choice to take a risk in spite of fear, it's not only the choice to act, but it's also an indication of strength of character. Now what if you decide to *not* act on something because you evaluated the risk and decided it wasn't worth it? Or you decided not to act in that particular moment because you realized something else needed to be done or happen first, which would make the risk more worthwhile in the future?

There are times that choosing inaction *instead* of action is just as courageous (and smart) because you're taking into account the importance of risk prevention and risk mitigation and deciding what its worth is to you. It's the soul-searching part of the choice that really matters, and this is where you'll learn how to develop deep trust in yourself.

Bravery, on the flip side, is the follow-through. It's all action, and having the guts and gumption to go and do what needs to be done, after you've decided on it. But, if you look up the definition of bravery on the wide world of the internet, it's going to tell you that bravery is what happens when you do something hard, painful, or dangerous in the absence of fear. I'm going to be that person who's willing to argue with the internet.

I've met many, many courageous and brave people in my life, and 100% of the time, when I ask them why they chose to do the big, scary thing that they went and did, they said, 'I decided it was worth it, and I just had to stop thinking about it and go and do it.'

From that perspective, dealing with fear, managing and tolerating risk, and being resilient, all become a conversation of choosing to do the big, scary thing without completely overthinking it. It turns into:

Evaluate -> Decide -> Do.

Until… you get tired.

Let's be honest.

Sometimes, life is going to be life. It's beautiful, but it's also a four-letter word.

We can sit here and talk all day about the things you need to learn, understand, and work at in order to build your ability to be resilient, but it's important to also remember that part of being resilient means knowing and embracing the reality that you can't run on empty.

The more tired you are, in any capacity, the less resilient you will become. Literally *everything* is harder when you're tired, and it's easy to get drained, straight down to your soul.

Resilience, and being resilient, demands that we show up to our lives with the willingness to check in with two questions:

1. What's my *ability* to do this thing?
2. What's my *capacity* to do this thing?

They're simple questions that become incredibly important gut checks that need to happen before pushing forward with a risk, or anything else for that matter. Capacity is going to ebb and flow for you, and your ebb-and-flow capacity is going to look different from the ebb and flow of other people. Your 50% may be someone else's 100%, just the same as another person's 100% may be your 150%. Capacity will be drained based on the amount of effort you're putting into something, and if you're really leaning into resilience, your capacity, and energy, will drain faster. Take the time to rest. It's not a failure to need to rest – it's being human, and it's wise to prioritize that.

I'm a mom, and a single mom at that. If you're in a parenting role, you know this shit ain't easy. That said, I like to think I'm a damn good mom. Not perfect, but damn good. My daughter and I are very close; we have some pretty ridiculous, silly moments together, and she knows I've got her back. Always. I feel both proud and confident in saying that my ability to 'mom' is on point – most days.

Except at night. Once the clock strikes 8:30pm, I start to want to pull a Cinderella and disappear under the comfort and solitude of my blankets, in my nice, comfy bed. I'm touched out, talked out, and worn out. I know, despite wanting my bedtime to be 8:30, it's going to be more like 10pm before I snuggle in for the night. So instead of 8:30 being my Cinderella moment, it becomes more like the dreaded 'witching hour' instead.

While my ability to do the 'mom' things that need to be done is always there, because my knowledge of how to do those things doesn't just vanish into thin air, my capacity to do those things is going to wax and wane with my energy levels.

It's the same for you, friend, and that's a-ok. You just have to remember to give yourself permission to let that be ok.

After all, you're a whole entire human being, packed with a whole entire identity, and resilience – along with all its puzzle pieces – is just a part of that.

RESILIENCE JOURNAL PROMPT

Take some time to examine where risk aversion and risk tolerance show up in your life and affect how resilient you feel in different situations. How does each one affect the choices you make, in how you deal with risk? Are there areas you can identify, where risk aversion holds you back from being more resilient? What do you feel ready, willing, and able to start doing differently to instead embrace the idea of risk tolerance in those areas?

3

IDENTITY

> ‘Here’s the key: I’m not going to tell you how to change. People don’t change. I want you to trust who you already are, and get to that Zone where you can shut out all the noise, all the negativity and fear and distractions and lies, and achieve whatever you want, in whatever you do.’
>
> — TIM S. GROVER, RELENTLESS: FROM GOOD TO GREAT TO UNSTOPPABLE

Trigger warning: This chapter contains my story of experiencing what I believed to be an abusive relationship. If this is a difficult topic for you, please either read it with a supportive person or skip to the section that starts with ‘Autophagy is...’.

If you are in a dangerous and/or abusive situation, please call the National Domestic Violence Hotline at: 1.800.799.7233

I asked you in the introduction if you could remember the last time someone asked you, 'Who are you?' Here's where we're going to dig into that question a whole lot more.

So, do you remember? If you do, do you remember how you answered?

Most of the time, most people are so caught up in the act of doing that it becomes extraordinarily simple to lose touch with what identity truly is. Instead, the idea of identity gets all twisted, and the focus shifts from *who* a person *is*, to *what* a person *does*. Stay in that space long enough, and eventually, you'll lose touch completely with who you actually are. Maybe you already have... I know I did, once upon a time.

The following story is about my experiences in what I perceived to be an abusive marriage, as well as my experiences in recovering from it. The skills and perspectives you'll find in this chapter are the same skills and perspectives I had to learn, practice, and create habits from, so that I could recover in a meaningful way. Exploring what it means to reconnect to your sense of identity means taking the time to understand the impact of what happened to you, and why you feel lost. From there, it's important to look inward and uncover the parts of you that were abandoned, while also looking forward to the future you want to create.

Before we proceed, I want to say this - I am proud of myself and my ex-husband, and where our relationship stands today. We co-parent our daughter well, respect each other's boundaries, and can communicate positively and constructively to accomplish goals and work as a team for the sake of our child. It wasn't always like that after the divorce, and it took a long time (and a lot of work) to get to this place. I'm proud of where we are and what we've been able to move through in our co-parenting relationship, for the sake of our daughter, for the sake of each other, and for the sake of peace.

I met my ex-husband in my early 20's. Being fresh out of my very first serious relationship, and feeling the sting of the breakup, he gave me the attention my insecure heart was desperately wanting. I had grown up feeling constantly like the proverbial ugly duckling – I was bullied by childhood friends and was often the butt of jokes in grade school. I had a massive growth spurt in the year between seventh and eighth grade, shooting up six inches and resulting in severe scoliosis. I needed surgery to correct it because one of the three curves in my spine was life-threatening. Today, I stand at 5'8", but if not for the scoliosis, I would have been 6' tall. I have a scar running the length of my entire back, from just below my neck and ending just above my hips. This scar became my nickname among the popular kids in eighth grade, straight through my freshman year of high school. During the start of puberty, at the height of all tweens' and teens' insecurities about their changing bodies and not knowing how the hell to deal with their emotions, I was dubbed 'Frankenstein'. It was just the *coolest*.

I believed, between the insecurities I had about my scoliosis and the scar, along with quite a few other things, that I was going to either be alone for the rest of my life, or I was going to have to take what I could get, because really – who would want a scarred-up, dorky kid like me?

I dismissed my knowledge and accomplishments all the time and only focused on what felt the worst. In spite of now recognizing as an adult (who's had a lot of therapy) that the people who loved me had only ever tried to encourage me, I only ever heard the criticisms and jokes. I never felt good enough, I never really felt like I fit in anywhere, and I found flaws in everything I tried or did. To say I became a perfectionist would be a generous understatement.

This eventually turned into a deep-seated need to be perfect on behalf of someone else - I started identifying myself through what I did and how other people perceived me, since it was all I could see.

When my ex and I met, it was easy for him to step into my life and become the hero I needed – someone who sang my praises, told me I was attractive, and actively voiced wanting to be in a relationship with me because of seeing positive, desirable qualities I had.

We started dating in 2004, got engaged in 2005, and got married in 2009. There were parts of the relationship that were genuinely good, and I truly loved being a wife. It meant something to me, having someone to come home to and to have someone come home to me, being able to care for that person and provide nurturing for their wants and needs, and feeling like my role really mattered for this person. I believed in my vows, and truly only ever wanted to say 'yes' once.

As much as there were parts of the relationship that were good, there were more parts that were really, really dark.

In spite of the good parts of the marriage, the dark parts were where I lost myself. We were married for almost five years, and throughout that time, no matter how unhappy I was, I put on a smile for the world and told everyone that everything was fine. I was absolutely convinced that, as a wife, it was my job to fix the issues we had because that was the role I had taken, and divorce wasn't an option I was willing to consider. I believed I was supposed to make him happy, and if I couldn't, it wasn't because he was doing something wrong or that the relationship was toxic – there was something wrong with me. I never set any boundaries that I actually stuck to, I stopped standing up for myself to the near-daily name-calling and mental games, I worked multiple jobs in order to financially keep us afloat after he quit his job on short notice without discussing it with me, and I worked my ass off despite not knowing what was going on with our finances or having a say in spending. I overfunctioned constantly, trying to compensate for where I felt I fell short. I was tired and overworked, my mental health was trash, and, after I gave birth to our daughter, I started to realize that I needed to leave the relationship. But I didn't know how.

During the last six months of the relationship, things suddenly escalated and I believed the threat of physical violence had become very real. I planned with my family how I would leave, and, one night, with my one-year-old daughter, a suitcase, and a garbage bag of toys in tow, I finally did it.

I knew, logically, that I couldn't stay married because of how the relationship was evolving. I perceived the environment I was in as no longer being safe, and felt almost constant fear for my physical well-being. But I was consumed by shame and feelings of failure about having to get divorced, because I believed my job was to fix the relationship, and I couldn't. I couldn't because it was never my responsibility to fix it on my own, and it never should have been my job to take ownership of things I felt he had created. My entire identity had been consumed by the relationship and the role of being a wife, and I knew I had to address it immediately.

There's a self-abandonment that sneaks in when we get so caught up in constantly doing and never being, constantly looking for the next thing without pausing to appreciate – or be concerned about – what's present already, and reacting impulsively and emotionally to our surroundings and relationships instead of slowing down and responding with thought and intention. It's even easier to self-abandon when you're already in a not-awesome headspace, because it'll take the eensiest, teeniest tap of a feather to push you over the edge and into the land of forgetting who you are. The stage had already been set for me when I got married, and it was absolutely simple to tip over into complete self-abandonment when I allowed myself to start existing for the sake of convenience to my ex-husband. Any of us can self-abandon, because it's just a reflection of how ridiculously easy it is to get lost in the perceptions and pressures of having to meet the expectations of the world around us. Our job is to make sure we keep those pressures in perspective so that we don't let them completely consume us.

Talking about being in any type of unsafe relationship or situation is never easy, and it certainly brings up a lot of really complicated and complex things for people. Taking a long, hard look at the messy shit any of us can go through is really difficult to tolerate, and it's easy to quickly get to the point of not wanting to look at it at all, thus avoiding it entirely and going right back into all our same old patterns. Regardless of what you feel stuck or lost in, you *have to* look at the messy shit if you want to change.

Autophagy is a medical term that describes the process our bodies go through to remove and recycle damaged or dysfunctional parts of a cell, so the body can then repair that cell. Neat, right? Our bodies come equipped with everything they need to repair themselves to maintain optimal function – as long as we take care of them.

In the process of leaving what I believed was an abusive relationship, I realized that autophagy can also be applied to the idea of identity.

The codependent, insecure, living-for-everyone-else-so-I-could-get-approval part of me needed to be removed and recycled so that I could uncover who I had always been, and then help that woman to start leveling up.

The process of autophagy, as applied to identity, requires two things: grief and psychological flexibility. Let's start with grief, because that's the 'removal' part of the autophagy process. You're going to have to grieve for the version of yourself that you're trying to leave behind, because that person doesn't fit in with the future you're trying to create. I couldn't be writing this book, running two successful businesses, and raising a badass kid if I allowed myself to remain codependent, insecure, and living on everyone else's terms. (Remember, fuck the rules. Write your own). I had to let that version of myself go and release her so she could stay in the past, while the new version of me stepped into the future. I know it sounds hippie-dippy and existential, but I promise this is important.

When it comes to grief, please also know there's no singular way to 'get it right' or 'get it wrong'. Grief is just... grief. You have to allow yourself time, space and permission to feel the messy feelings grief wants you to feel until they start to fade enough that you can move on. Being able to move on means taking the time to be present with what you're feeling – therapy is a great resource to use in the process of working through things like grief, because trying to do this solo can sometimes be a really big (and confusing) task.

Once you've removed what's no longer useful, then you have to recycle. This is where psychological flexibility comes into play. This concept has been studied and defined in some pretty complicated ways – let's simplify it a bit, shall we?

Being psychologically flexible means you can hang out in the present moment and stay aware of your thoughts and emotions – even (and especially) the crappy ones – so you can practice working on accepting them instead of judging or avoiding them. It's staying in the moment, instead of checking out. When you're able to do this, no matter how uncomfortable it is, you all of a sudden start giving yourself the chance to learn from the past. This is where you've got to be a bit like Gumby. Stay flexible, friend.

We're able to learn from the past when we stop beating ourselves up over the past. If I had stayed in a mental space of living in shame about being divorced, mortified that I experienced what I felt should be labeled as abuse - despite being a therapist - and having all the 'I should know better' thoughts, I never would have learned the lessons I needed to learn so I could become who I am today.

The same can be said for any of us. The longer you allow yourself to avoid, deny, blame, pretend, or just 'keep on, keepin' on', well, friend... Nothing changes if nothing changes.

In allowing myself to grieve for the 'me' who got into a bad situation, I started to feel compassion for that version of myself. When that compassion started to grow, that's when it became far easier to start practicing psychological flexibility, and ask 'What do I need to learn from this experience?' instead.

The same can be said for you – start by allowing yourself to grieve for the parts or version of you that need(s) to be left in the past. They don't serve a purpose in the future you're going to create. As you grieve, notice where the compassion for that old version of you starts to form, and go looking for the lessons your past has been trying to teach you.

For me, the lessons in identity became:

1. There's a big difference between being victimized and being a victim. One is a statement of fact, while the other is a mindset.

2. Rock-solid boundaries protect the most sacred parts of my life. And, they are non-negotiable.
3. My wants and needs matter just as much as anyone else's and deserve to be honored.
4. I always have permission to leave a place that's no longer serving me.
5. I will forever be a key person of influence in my life.

Let's pay attention to that last point.

Go to Google and ask it about 'Key Person of Influence', and you'll get almost one billion hits about this idea and what it means. This is an idea that started out in the business world, and what it both means and takes to rise to the top tier of your industry. But we can apply this idea much more broadly, too.

Being a key person of influence in your own life really is about understanding the approach you take to how and why you live life the way you do, and is your belief on why that matters. This can be super helpful, but it can also be super toxic. That's going to depend on you.

I was as much a key person of influence in my life during my marriage as I am now, but the difference lies in the perspective. I used to believe that it was my responsibility to live on behalf of others and provide for their comfort (*super toxic*), and I now believe it is my responsibility to keep myself as healthy and whole as possible so that I can create a legacy for myself and my daughter that is both empowering and inspiring. The amount of influence in each perspective is the same, but the *quality* of influence in each perspective is wildly different.

And that's the point about perspective. You get to choose. Powerful, right?

The combination of choice and perspective is a formidable tool. It reminds me of the choose-your-own adventure books I used to love when I was a kid. I was a voracious reader of these books, along with all things fairy-tale, Nancy Drew, and Carmen Sandiego (And, of course, a bit of Babysitter's Club, too. Why not?). The choose-your-own adventure books always intrigued me the most. I'd get three at a time from the librarian; she'd give me her sideways smile and a wink, and off I'd go. Within a few days, I would read each one, intentionally choosing a different path through the book each time until I had read it from every possible angle. I loved it, because it felt like there were two or three different books hidden on the pages in front of me, just waiting to be discovered and explored.

In many ways, life really is no different than one of these books. We all experience a myriad of different things. For some, it can be a series of heartache after heartache with seemingly no end. For others, it's joy on top of joy, on top of joy. And yet others, it's a bit of all of the above. The 'choose your own adventure' part comes into play when you decide to take the reins and start controlling the impact you allow these experiences to have on you and how you feel about yourself.

Remember, you are *informed* by your experiences. Your identity doesn't ever have to be *defined* by them. That's the beauty of choice.

After growing to believe I was in a hostile relationship and choosing to leave it, it would have been so ridiculously easy for me to live in a space of being angry at myself and the world, stuck in a never-ending shame spiral, blaming not only myself, but everyone and everything else for my problems, and more. It would have been easy to stay stuck in a fixed mindset, never having to practice resilience, and allowing my identity to stay lost in my past. If I had allowed that, not only would I have been picking up and continuing what I felt was the abuse (where my ex left off), but I would have been forced to pay the price of staying small and never really discovering who I could have been.

While staying the same may be comfortable because the space of smallness is familiar, it's also a space of suffering and staying lost.

On the other hand, there's also a price tag attached to change. Let's acknowledge here that this cost will look different for each person – we all have different tolerance levels for cost and have different support systems that affect what costs we can afford to take on. What's the cost of becoming the person you most desire to be: your truest self? The price I had to pay was ending my marriage and learning how to swallow my pride while asking for help as a single parent, along with realizing which relationships and friendships I needed to leave behind. It wasn't that those people weren't valuable – they were, and still are. It was simply that they did not fit in with the future I was working on creating.

I also paid the price, in effort, of doing some really, really hard shit, starting with leaving my marriage while building my first business. When we do hard things, delaying that instant gratification we all crave, we build patience. We also build tenacity and mental toughness. It is in embracing the value of 'hard' that your truest self, the person you desire to be, is built and then revealed.

It was scary, hard, overwhelming, and sometimes painful to become who I am today. But it was ***also*** joyful, hopeful, exhilarating, hella fun, and wildly, massively empowering to become present-day me. Just as there would have been a big price tag attached to staying the same, there was also a price tag attached to change – and it was *worth it*.

Dealing with the cost of change, especially when it comes to expansion, leveling up in life, or whatever you want to call it, is worth it more often than not, but it's especially important and worth it when it comes to your sense of identity and belief in who you are.

Having a strong sense of self is a reflection of confidence in knowing yourself, what you're capable of, what you believe you do and don't deserve, being meaningfully connected to people you value and who also challenge you, and more. You'll catch yourself seeking validation a whole lot less and really not living on other people's terms anymore, because that strong sense of self doesn't require confirmation from other people. When you know yourself, you learn how to trust yourself.

While all of us are complex creatures, there's a simple way to start the process of getting to know you. It's all about understanding the difference between roles, labels, and identity. Let's discuss.

First, let's define each one. Defining what roles are in your life is pretty black and white: your roles are only ever things that you do. Now please don't take that as me saying your roles don't matter – it's quite the opposite, actually. I'm a mom, and that's the absolute most important role I play. Being a mom takes up at least 70% of my life, and I'm absolutely cool with that because I chose it and my kid rocks. But despite that, being a mom is still only ever something that I do. It's not who I am. We're brought up believing that our roles, because of the amount of time they often require and the influence they have in our lives, are the things we're supposed to define ourselves according to. I couldn't disagree more. It's absolutely ok to give a role you play a place of importance, if you so choose, but defining who you are according to that role sticks you very quickly in a place of being one-dimensional, when you are so much more than that.

Labels are a little more grey than roles. Labels are ways the world describes you, based on how other people experience you. These could be things like:

woman/man/non-binary
white/black/Asian/islander/indigenous
rich/poor/middle-class

independent/strong/resilient
kind/compassionate/caring
asshole/bitchy/mean

Labels can be confusing for people, because sometimes they're based on fact (such as, I am biologically female and present as such, so people will label me as a woman because of my appearance), and sometimes they're based on opinion. If you're having an off day, and someone approaches you with a question or a need, maybe you're going to snap at them. It's not that they did anything wrong, and they may have nothing to do with why you're having an off day. But snapping at them could result in them labeling you as bitchy or as being an asshole in that moment. Does that mean that's actually who you are, or does that mean that you're simply having a bad day and they happened to have the bad luck of running into you? It's important to understand the difference between how we're perceived by the world around us and what influences those perceptions, versus who we actually are. Without keeping perspective on that, it's easy to fall into the trap of starting to believe that our labels – especially the negative ones – are actually who we are when they may not be.

Now here's the good stuff. We've talked roles and labels, and now it's all about identity. Identity is never black and white – that's first and important to understand. Identity is about eleventy-seven different shades of grey, because that's how complex and nuanced we all are. Identity is a collection of beliefs, quirks and characteristics, values, experiences, and so, so much more. These things come together to shape who you are, why you behave the way you do, why your perspectives, opinions, and beliefs are how they are, and why you do things the specific way you do them. Let's talk through some examples.

If we look at two different women who are mothers, they're both playing the same role. But if one woman is religious, while the other is spiritual, these women all of a sudden have a very distinct difference that shows up in their belief system. One is not better or worse than the other – they're just two different sets of beliefs in a higher power. Where this becomes important is in how those beliefs show up when each woman is actively parenting her children. The religious woman may have beliefs about the importance of her children receiving the sacraments, while the spiritual woman may teach her children about why valuing their land and connecting with nature is important. Neither woman is wrong in how she's parenting her children, but they will engage in their role of being a mother in two really different ways because of their beliefs. This is why the roles we play in our lives are never who we are; but who we are informs the way we show up to engage in those roles.

Now if we look at personality quirks and characteristics, you could have two people who you have to do separate projects with. One is extremely stubborn, knows exactly what they want, they have clear ideas about what they believe is important in that project, and they're vocal about their boundaries and expectations of working as a team. The other person is generally very easy-going, always saying they're happy to just 'go with the flow'. They love your suggestions about the project you're assigned to together, and, because of that, they rarely offer suggestions of their own. They're quite pleased with the idea of following your lead, and encourage you to be in a leadership role during the project. Based off these personality quirks and characteristics, which person would you rather work with on a project? How would you label each person? Some people may label Person One as a leader because they're obviously comfortable stepping into a leadership role and have no problem making themselves heard. Other people, however, may view Person One as headstrong, controlling, and bossy because of how they speak up for themselves and their ideas. On the other hand, people may label Person Two as fun, laid-back, and easy to work with because of their nonchalant attitude. But, they could also be labeled as frustrating, lazy, flaky, and unreliable. It's important to be aware of your personality quirks and characteristics, because when other people experience them, this is where your labels will come from.

Do you see in those examples how much identity influences and impacts what our roles and labels end up looking like? Identity is a far more powerful and important thing than we often give it credit for, and it's a potent tool in shaping how you both show up to the world and experience the world around you.

At the start of this chapter, I asked you when the last time was that someone asked you: 'Who are you?'

If you don't remember, let this be that moment. I'm asking, and I want to know all about who you are, what makes you tick the way you do, and what all the glorious, complicated, complex, messy, exciting, beautiful, frustrating, and goofy parts of you are. The process of exploring the depths of who you are can be overwhelming and scary at first – just let that be. After a while, the overwhelming and scary starts to fade as you begin discovering all your different parts and pieces and start fitting them together. Then, what you're left with is a whole lot of fun in discovering the rest of the puzzle pieces that make you, you.

And, after all, you are absolutely worthy and deserving of discovering the entirety of the masterpiece of who you are.

IDENTITY JOURNAL PROMPT

Make a list of the things you feel apply to you, under each category of Roles, Labels, and Identity. As you're writing, notice how you feel about the parts that come easily and the parts that may be more of a struggle. Do you know yourself as well as you thought you did? How does each category impact the way you lead your life and make choices for your life?

4

INTEGRITY

> 'We control our actions, but the consequences that flow from those actions are controlled by principles.'
>
> — DR. STEPHEN COVEY

I'll never forget him:

Dressed in a t-shirt, jeans, and basic kicks, with a beard and sideburns that could win awards, John was a guy that, upon first sight, you immediately knew you wanted not only to be buddies with, but you *really* wanted to have him on your side.

As a retired special forces soldier, he carried himself with the confidence of a man who knew how dark the world could be and chose to be happy anyway. His face was plastered constantly with the goofiest smile, and he had the most 'dad' sense of humor out of any guy I've ever known. And yet, when it was time to get to work and learn how to protect yourself, John was all business.

I met John in 2015 when I signed up for a series of self-defense classes he was running. These classes were important to me and played a big role in learning how to feel safe in the world again after leaving my marriage, but what I didn't expect were the lessons I got about integrity, values, and what it meant to stay in alignment.

John, constantly flanked by his co-instructors, moved fluidly from lesson to lesson for weeks, teaching me and my classmates different strategies, perspectives, and defensive tactics. His co-instructors would move through the room we always met in, sometimes partnering with me and my fellow classmates, sometimes taking over teaching while John attended to other things, but always moving with an air of deference towards John and the role he had in all of our lives.

And that's just the thing: this deference I saw among John's co-instructors wasn't just humble submission because John was the boss. It was true respect, not just because of *what* John was, but because of *who* John was.

Watching him for weeks and how he interacted with all the people around him, John was a walking, talking, breathing masterclass in values and practicing self-leadership through alignment.

John had this absolute, unshakable belief in how much people deserve to be free and to be safe. He told story after story throughout each class about the people he met during his military career, the teams he worked with, and how happy it made him to be able to defend the innocent, no matter what it meant he might have to do. (John really loved being a soldier. Like, *really* loved it.) He was unwavering in what he believed it meant to 'do the right thing'. And that was John's 'why'. It was the first time I had a front-row seat to truly watch someone live for a purpose, on purpose.

Years later, in the process of learning about purpose, vision, and mission statements in the business world, I got to thinking: what if this is actually just a really important part of living well? Let's break it down.

In the business world, companies use purpose, vision, and mission statements to keep businesses focused on the overall goals the business was created to achieve. Think of it this way:

- Purpose = Why. This is the reason the business exists in the first place.
- Vision = What. This is what the business is trying to achieve or create in the future, in order to fulfill its 'Why'.
- Mission = How. This is the roadmap the business follows as it works on achieving the 'What' and 'Why'.

John's purpose, or his 'Why', was the belief that people should be able to live freely and safely. His vision, or his 'What', then became his desire to see people bravely standing up for themselves, and he did this through teaching self-defense classes after he retired from the military. The classes became his mission, or his 'How'.

Everything that John was, was shaped around his purpose, vision, and mission. His values, beliefs, morality, world views, actions, and more, all became direct extensions of these guiding principles. It was his identity, but it was also so much more.

Now I know this is deep. But to live well, you need to know what you're living for.

I found my purpose – my 'Why' – in the process of leaving my marriage. It was the most disempowered and uninspired time of my life, where I felt constantly trapped, so I made the decision, in leaving, that I would always live freely while working at empowering and inspiring the people around me. I literally just chose the opposite of what I had experienced.

Here's the thing, though: your 'Why' doesn't have to come from some deep, dark place in your life. Not everything has to be part of the 'Big Bad', after all. It's a perfectly acceptable thing for your purpose to be found in joyful experiences, such as becoming a parent, landing your dream job with your dream salary, prioritizing self-care before anything else, or being totally consumed by an awesome case of wanderlust. All that matters is that you're able to identify a 'Why' that holds meaning for you, and fully own it.

According to Merriam-Webster, integrity is defined as:

> 'Firm adherence to a code of especially moral or artistic values.'

When it comes to developing and practicing integrity, having a strong 'Why' is step one, and practicing radical ownership as part of self-leadership is step two.

In the book 'Extreme Ownership: How U.S. Navy SEALs Lead and Win', retired SEALs Jocko Willink and Leif Babin provide example after example of how the SEALs teach and then practice leadership and ownership. Over and over again, they preach one simple principle about what it means to not only practice leadership, but to take ownership when something goes wrong. They say:

 "Leadership is simple, but not easy."

I couldn't agree more. The simplicity of something is really just a matter of logistics, but we complicate the shit out of most things because instead of just focusing on doing what needs to be done, we get all messy and emotional about it. This is where people get off track. Now don't get me wrong here, your emotions absolutely matter – they have a place, there's no emotion that's wrong or bad, and it's an essential part of the human experience to feel the feels (probably more often than you really want to...) – but it's important to also recognize the impact your emotions have on your behavior.

It is so freaking normal to struggle with just owning our crap, because we get:

- Embarrassed
- Ashamed
- Overwhelmed by it

- Angry at ourselves
- Frustrated
- Sad
- Anxious

Fun, right? <*Not*> So when all these emotions come up that no one actually wants to spend time feeling, it only stands to reason that any one of us would go straight into avoidance mode. No one wants to feel shitty about themselves, after all.

And yet in order to actually practice self-leadership and ownership, taking a long, hard look at the things we feel both joy about and less-than-stellar about is a thing that does need to happen.

Every single time you practice integrity by standing firm in your 'Why' and taking ownership over the good, the bad, and the ugly in your life without trying to avoid it, you're building and reinforcing more parts of who you are. Practicing integrity is a character-building and character-shaping experience, because it requires you to hold your head high and claim the very ground you stand on, when what you really want to do is run and hide.

When you actively practice self-leadership in this way, the people around you are going to notice – whether you want them to or not. And I know you know that when people notice, people talk. This is where reputations are born.

When you let your character lead the way by planting your flag firmly on your 'Why', practicing self-leadership through staying true to who you are, and taking radical ownership over your life, your reputation will naturally become what you want it to be.

Talking about integrity means having to also talk about the side-effects of integrity. Parts and pieces of this are things we've already touched on: having a strong 'Why', practicing self-leadership, taking radical ownership over your life, and allowing those things to shape your character and reputation.

Another integrity side-effect, though, is humility. It would have been easy to wrap that up into less than one sentence while talking about character, but operating with humility is so important that it deserves its own spot.

This saying has become one of the guideposts for my life, as it's shown up over and over again:

> 'Never be the smartest person in the room. If you are, find a different room.'

There are a lot of super cool, powerful, thought-provoking quotes and sayings about why operating with humility is so important, but this one has always hit home for me. I hope it does for you, too.

For most people, the idea of operating with humility seems like common sense. I mean, no one is purposefully going out into the world with the intention of acting like a self-involved asshole, right? (We're going to sit here and hope so.)

If humility is such a common-sense idea, then why do we see people struggling with it so much? It's a difficult question to answer, because there isn't just one singular reason. People have learned how to live at extremes throughout the generations that have roamed this weird, blue-floating-space ball we call Earth. For some, operating with humility gets taken to such an extreme that they end up being literally their own worst enemy, stuck in seemingly endless cycles of self-deprecation and thinking they're just the *worst.* (Sound familiar?) Yet for others, their humility seems to get sucked into a void of nonexistence and then they actually *become* the worst, thinking that just because they succeeded in one thing, they're now God's Gift (when really they're just a one-hit-wonder). Both sides of that equation involve having to change the way we view ourselves, which – just like leadership – is simple, but not necessarily easy.

I've found over and over again that correcting the way we view ourselves needs to start by looking at ourselves as students. This is where the saying 'Never be the smartest person in the room' becomes important.

Look at it this way: if you're the smartest person in the room, you're going to start believing there's nothing left for you to learn, accomplish, conquer, or achieve. This is where egos start to get out of control, but this is also where people can start to become lazy, because being 'the smartest' births this belief that there's nothing worthwhile left to do.

But if you put yourself in the position of being a student, there's a challenge to that role. Being a student means:

1. There's always something left that's still worthwhile for you to do or learn.
2. You have to pay attention to the people, places, and things you're surrounded by.
3. You get to learn what you do and don't expect of yourself, along with what you're willing to accept, in relation to what and who you're surrounded by.
4. There's value in mentorship, no matter what level you've climbed to personally and professionally.

Throughout my life and careers, I've met a lot of people who were a hell of a lot smarter than me. Two of these people were my very first EMT instructors, and the lessons they taught me still influence what I do today. They were a husband-and-wife team who were larger than life. They were unbelievably intimidating because of the confidence and authority they carried themselves with, but despite that, they were also two of the most gentle, kindest human beings I've had the privilege of learning from and calling my friends. Just like my self-defense instructor John was respected, I had (and still have) deep respect for my EMT instructors.

During class one day, they hollered out this lesson of never being the smartest person in the room. It started a big discussion between all the instructors and my classmates about why, in the emergency services, it was actually dangerous to think you're 'the smartest'. Stories were shared by the instructors about past partners they had worked with who let their egos get out of control, and then became complacent in their patient care. The instructors shared how painful it was for them to see these partners end up hurting people they were responsible for, and how, in more cases than not, it ended either with serious harm to a patient, or it ended the person's career. The point of needing to constantly learn, take in more information, and always work on improving, no matter how much we knew, was emphasized over and over again.

While I continued to have other people like John enter my life to teach me new lessons and reinforce old ones, the lesson of never being the smartest person in the room started in my time in EMS.

The tricky part about humility is staying humble enough to continue to always learn, while also not minimizing the things you do know and the ways you're accomplished. Practicing kindness towards ourselves and feeling proud of what we've accomplished keeps us from going to the extreme of humility where we become our own worst enemy, while actively looking to learn from others and maintaining that 'student mindset', keeps us from going to the other extreme where humility is overtaken by ego. It takes time, attention, and effort to balance these ideas out, and to realize that after a certain point, it is possible to be both the student and the teacher. As you learn how to balance these ideas and stay more and more in touch with your values over time, living with integrity becomes second nature.

'Life can only be understood backwards; but it must be lived forwards.'

— SOREN KIERKEGAARD

It's impossible to learn about integrity and its side-effects of having a strong 'Why', practicing radical ownership, staying humble, leading with character, and building reputation without also thinking about the things you've experienced in your life.

It can be both comforting and challenging to look backward and find the lessons life has thrown your way, but to move forward and live well, this is a necessary practice.

I first learned about this through being an EMT. The nature of working in the emergency services is... well... tough. There are things emergency services personnel have to do over the course of their shifts and careers that are just simply not normal to do. There's a constant exposure to the underbelly of society, and, for most first responders, it changes the way they view the world. I know it certainly did for me.

After responding to a difficult incident, debriefings always happen. Sometimes they're very formal and spread across multiple departments that were all involved in the incident, but more often than not, debriefings are very informal and are done on a crew's own terms. In ten years of being in EMS, I was involved in two formal debriefings, and hundreds of informal ones. The informal ones were my favorite, and always were the ones I found the most helpful. There was just something about sitting in the cab of the ambulance with my partner, taking a collective breath, and having a 'what the fuck just happened' moment before we started to process the call we had just done.

It was often hard to talk about these experiences, but in talking I always found relief. Being able to talk about what went right and what went wrong, how we felt about what we just saw and did, and talk about what we could have done differently or what we felt proud of – it was necessary and unbelievably helpful in reinforcing both what we were really fucking good at, versus what we needed to pay more attention to next time.

Eventually, I became a training officer and started training both EMT students and new employees for the company I was with. After every call, I'd sit my trainee down and we'd talk about what we did, how they felt, and what worked versus what didn't. Those conversations were just as important and necessary for me as they were for my trainees, because they always highlighted what I needed to continue to work on as an instructor so I could best help the people I was teaching.

Learning about debriefings, being a part of them, and experiencing the impact of them taught me the importance of doing my own debriefings about my personal life. In the work I do with my clients, we regularly talk about the idea of doing a personal debrief, which can show up in so many different ways. You can go to therapy, journal about it, have a vulnerable conversation with a trusted friend, and more. There isn't a 'wrong' way to debrief, as long as you're examining the past so you can learn from it and move forward productively. This matters because reflection is integral to integrity.

Here's the most important part of this: you're not ever going to look back and find something that was absolutely, utterly perfect. Flaws and fuckups will always exist, because that's a normal, necessary part of the human experience. It's important to not beat yourself up for those things or hyperfocus on them to the point that you can't see anything else (which is certainly easier said than done, but still important). When you look for the lesson the flaw or fuckup is trying to teach you, you'll start to recover faster and faster (resilience!), moving forward with your life in a stronger, more intelligent, more values-aligned way each time.

So what does it mean to live in alignment with your values?

When you take the time to really examine who you believe you are, what you say you value, and whether or not you're living from a place of true integrity, you start the process of creating a set of guardrails that help you stay on track with living well. Without those guardrails, it's stupid-easy to get all sorts of caught up in what you think other people want from you, falling into patterns that are wildly unhelpful, and forgetting entirely about the things that matter most to you.

There are examples all over the place of what it looks like to have a simple, yet strong, set of guardrails for your life. One of my favorites comes from the teachings of Don Miguel Ruiz, who wrote the book 'The Four Agreements'.

The Agreements are:

1. Be impeccable with your word.
2. Don't take anything personally.
3. Don't make assumptions.
4. Always do your best.

Simple, right?

The simplicity is on purpose, and it matters so much more than you may realize. When you get caught up with living in this ultra-complicated, on-everyone-else's-terms, self-sacrificial way, everything starts to feel hard, overwhelming, and messy. When you slow down and check in with yourself and your values, you start having the chance to get back in line with what really matters: *you*. And that's really what alignment and living with integrity is all about.

From there, it's just a matter of training so that you keep the skills, knowledge, and self-awareness you've worked so hard for.

INTEGRITY JOURNAL PROMPT

Start getting back in touch with you and your integrity. Write down your purpose, vision, and mission: what is it about these things that matters to you and for you? If you notice that you want to have different sets of these statements for different parts of your life, that's also ok – go with your gut and trust your instincts.

5

TRAINING

'Tell me and I forget, teach me and I may remember, involve me and I may learn.'

— BENJAMIN FRANKLIN

Training isn't just about what you can do with your body; it's also about what you can do with your mind.

Every single thing we've touched on so far – growth, resilience, identity, and integrity – aren't just ideas. They're *skills*; and skills require persistent training.

Here's the thing: we're taught that once we learn something, we have the information forever and we no longer need to put effort into how we apply that information. This is only sort of right, and mostly wrong, unfortunately.

You see, knowledge and intelligence are two wildly different things. Knowledge is simply a measure of the information you know, while intelligence is your ability to apply that information in a meaningful way. Just because you know something doesn't mean you possess the intelligence to apply that knowledge. Now that also doesn't mean you're a dummy – not by a long shot, friend. It means there's a skill set that you have yet to learn, or there's a skill set that was allowed to atrophy, just like a muscle can atrophy. Let's break this down by using CrossFit as an example.

I walked into my very first CrossFit class back in 2017. I was the 'new kid' in class, and even though all eyes were not actually on me, you bet your bottom dollar it sure felt like they were. I was afraid of making a fool of myself, but I wanted the accountability of showing up to a class so I could work on my health. I knew I liked lifting weights, but I also knew I hated running and all things cardiovascular, so CrossFit seemed like a perfect mix of things I could jam out on and things I would be challenged by. Running basically feels like my equivalent of medieval torture, and while I dreaded that part of the class, I was ready to figure out how far I could push my limits. So there I went. And let me tell you, the strength portion of the classes was *un-freaking-believably* fun! Over the course of my time with the group I took classes with, I quickly caught up with them strength-wise, but I was the slogger (slow jogger, for my un-punny peeps) of the group. It ended up being completely ok that I was always the slowest, and I was certainly always challenged to find my limits and push past them.

Eventually, my budget and time commitments changed, and I had to stop going to this class I had fallen in love with. I was bummed, but I was able to collect enough gym equipment (Facebook Marketplace for the win!!) so that I could continue at least some of the workouts at home. I had gained the knowledge of how to lift weights properly during my time at CrossFit, but didn't have the same amount of room to move around, since I was now exercising primarily in my basement. There were certain types of lifts I just literally didn't have the overhead room to do properly or safely, so I stopped doing them.

I continued to exercise those muscle groups in other ways in order to maintain the muscle I had gained, but I lost the confidence to perform the actual CrossFit movements properly and safely on my own because I chose to not train on them anymore. I'd exercise outside periodically and still wouldn't do them. I wouldn't do them, because mindset, confidence, and resilience are *perishable skills*. This is where the saying 'If you don't use it, you lose it' really applies.

When we start to realize how quickly we can lose the skills we need in order to truly live well, it's no wonder it's so easy for any of us to get stuck. Persistent training takes intention, time, dedication to consistency, and more, but when we're constantly caught up in the 'busy' of life, it's unbelievably easy to lose perspective on the things we say we value and desire. It's also silly easy to get caught up in the assumptions of 'I'll get to it one day; I just have to get through this *thing* first', or 'I just need to clear my plate a little and then I'll have time', or better (or worse) yet, 'I want that *thing* so badly, but I'm just kidding myself – I can't actually be successful with it'.

Do any of those sound familiar? If you notice yourself getting caught up in saying those kinds of things, consider it normal.

This is a not-so-fun phenomenon called 'Immunity to Change'. This phenomenon, coined by Harvard Graduate School of Education Professor Robert Kegan and Lecturer Lisa Lahey, essentially says that despite deeply desiring change, human beings also have an aversion to change. We fill our minds with all these negative assumptions about why we can't change, despite desperately wanting to, basically because we're terrified to fail or fuck it all up. Isn't being a human just *the best*? (I promise it's ok to roll your eyes at that - I'm rolling mine, too.)

In their research and in the programs they've since launched to help people better understand their resistance to change (despite seriously wanting to change), Kegan and Lahey explain that people often fail to achieve their goals and make the changes they want because they focus only on behavioral change. While behavioral change matters, it's only one half of the whole shebang. The other half of creating real change rests in addressing the changes needed in a person's mindset and addressing those negative assumptions any of us can pull out of thin air. This is why training mindset, resilience, and making sure you're consistently checking in with your view of yourself and what you value matters so much.

When you train consistently on leveling up your mindset, it's going to challenge you to identify the blind spots you didn't know you had. Dr. Eliyahu Goldratt, a leader in business management, first introduced the 'Theory of Constraints' in his book 'The Goal'. If you've ever heard the saying 'the chain is only as strong as its weakest link', the Theory of Constraints is all about figuring out how to not only identify which link in that chain is actually the weakest, but how to manage that link so that the chain doesn't break.

Two of the blind spot 'weak links' in your chain come from, ironically enough, starting to feel better. They're called 'Salience Bias', and 'The Arrival Fallacy'. Let's look at Salience Bias first.

Social psychologist Shelley Taylor was among the first group of people to begin discussing the concept of salience and the impact it has on our mindset and perceptions of the people and the world around us. In psychology, 'Salience Bias' refers to the idea that we tend to only focus on the parts of something that are the most obvious or stand out the most. By focusing only on the things that stand out the most about someone or an experience, salience acts as a sort of filter. This helps us to not get completely overloaded with information as we work on different tasks or goals. Sounds great, right? (It's sort of great, but also sort of not)

If salience acts as a filter, and you're working towards this super cool goal you've been chipping away at, it starts to feel more and more exciting. The closer you get to the goal, the end line starts to be all you can see and focus on. Have you ever stopped to notice, though, what happens to your motivation as you get closer to a goal? For most people, motivation drops *way* off when they think they're about to achieve something. And this, my friend, is the impact of 'The Arrival Fallacy'.

Named by psychologist Tal Ben-Shahar, 'The Arrival Fallacy' is the idea that we'll finally be happy once we achieve a certain goal. The combination of this fallacy with salience leaves us feeling more excited about achieving a goal the closer we get to it, because we start only focusing on what we think achieving the goal is going to make us feel like. When that happens, because of the filter of salience, it's easy to stop focusing on the work that still has to happen to achieve the goal, our motivation drops as a result, our effort at doing the work drops off, and then... we don't end up achieving the goal. Big bummer.

Now salience is part of human nature. We're hardwired to focus on specific things for specific reasons, and we're not going to undo that. But we can certainly harness it, train it, and use it to our advantage. Instead of focusing so much on how achieving a goal is going to make us feel, we can train ourselves to use salience instead to focus on the process of achieving a goal. Most of the time, we skip right over the impact of going through the process of working towards something. The more we do that, though, the more we skip over the really juicy, extra good parts of life. When we prioritize focusing on the process of working towards the goal, we're focusing on why training can be just as enjoyable as meeting the goal, if not more enjoyable. Think about it like savoring the journey <u>AND</u> the destination.

If you're working towards losing a whole bunch of weight, and you're only focusing on the end result, you're going to miss the chance to really celebrate all the milestones you achieve along the way. And that's the point. The milestones we hulk-smash through on the way to achieving the goal are far, far more important than the actual goal, because they represent all the ways we're changing. We're focusing on the training over/in addition to the goal, just as we've been told to savor the journey, not (just) the destination.

Meredith Root and Alex Parker, owners of Tactic Functional Nutrition (find them on Instagram, @tacticnutrition – it's an awesome account to follow!), said in a post about effort and training:

> "Have expectations of effort, not outcome.
>
> Life will give you nothing.
>
> Just because you show up and take up space doesn't mean you'll get what you want. And a fast track to frustration is believing you should be in a better situation than you are. It's having expectations of an outcome.
>
> Expectations can be a good thing but only when you have expectations of yourself and your own effort. That's it. Hold yourself to a high standard of behavior and grit. Have expectations that you will show up the next day even when you get the shit kicked out of you or you fail, or you struggle, or you're embarrassed. That's the process. That's how you grow.
>
> If you can maintain that expectation of effort, the outcome tends to take care of itself."

What Alex and Meredith (and yours truly) are saying is that the importance of the *process* of 'doing the work' (i.e., training) outweighs the *outcome* of 'doing the work', alwaysandforeverthankyouamen. I mean it.

 'But KELLY! I still *need* a goal... What do I do?!'

Pay attention here, I never said to stop setting goals. Goals, after all, do matter as part of training. Having something exciting to work towards is fun, it gets us motivated to swing into action, and it keeps us focused on the future. Those things are important, and we need all those parts and more.

Goals will always matter, but:

1. You need better, more organized goals.

2. Setting and working towards goals means balancing out:

- Being able to stay in the moment long enough to celebrate the wins you collect on the way to achieving your goals, and
- Looking towards the future and what you're trying to achieve or accomplish.

It's all about balance, baby. Balance.

So how do we set better goals? We get SMART about it, and weave in the things we value. Let's talk about SMART goals.

The idea of SMART goals was first introduced in a paper written by George T. Doran in 1981, when he wrote about how important it was for managers to write better goals and objectives for their departments. He defined SMART goals as being:

Specific
Measurable
Achievable
Relevant
Time-bound

If you think about how you normally set goals, you're probably hitting a couple of these points, but likely also missing some. Unless you've been taught about goal setting somewhere in your past, it's incredibly common to not know how to set a goal in a really specific way. Here's two examples for how a SMART goal can look:

1. Having a better relationship with a romantic partner:

Specific: I want to build a better relationship with my partner, where we both feel our needs are acknowledged and met more consistently.

Measurable: We will schedule date nights weekly, in order to create a closer connection.

Attainable: We already have the time available for date nights, because we have an established babysitter (if you have children) and we spend most nights just sitting on the couch, watching TV or staring at our phones.

Relevant: My relationships have always been important to me, and the closer I am to the people I love, the more loved and valued I also feel.

Time-bound: I will have a conversation with my partner tonight about this goal and schedule our first date night before the end of this week.

2. ***Managing emotions more effectively:***

Specific: I will learn how to control my emotions more effectively, which will in turn help me to feel more calm, confident, and in control of myself.

Measurable: I will write in my journal every night, and use a mood tracking app daily so I can see where I'm making progress and where I still need to focus more.

Attainable: Journaling and using apps are usually low-cost, accessible, and don't take up a ton of time. I've also been practicing mindfulness for the last couple of years, so I can recognize when I need to write something down.

Relevant: People have been giving me feedback that my emotions have been worrying them because I've been more up and down lately than I've been in the past.

Time-bound: I'm up for a promotion at work in the next couple of months, and I know that I could lose that promotion if I don't learn how to manage my stress and anxiety more effectively.

See how that works? Setting goals isn't just about identifying a point way out yonder that you think might make you feel good; it's about: (S) being crystal clear about what you want and why you want it, (M) deciding both a frequency for the effort you'll put towards achieving the goal, along with how you'll know when the goal is met, (A) knowing all the factors that need to be in place for that thing to happen, (R) whether or not it's actually realistic to achieve that thing or if maybe there's something else that needs to happen first, and (T) giving yourself a deadline. To set goals well, you have to get way more specific than you think you need to. Without that, it's like pissing into the wind and hoping you don't get wet. It just doesn't work. And, that's gross. Please don't do that.

Once you've got the goal you're excited about, it's time to turn straight back to putting in effort through consistent training. Remember, the goal matters, but the effort and training you put in matters more.

We all put in effort all the time, all day long. But do you ever stop and think about whether or not you're putting in effort on the 'right' things? As I write this sentence, it's 10:24pm. I'm aware that I need to vacuum my house, do the paperwork for therapy sessions I've held this week, get a load of my daughter's laundry done, clean up my dog's tennis balls that she strategically hid all over the house over the course of the day today (because I'd rather not step on one in the dark, go flying, and break my damn neck), pay my quarterly taxes like a good little entrepreneur who wants to stay friends with the IRS, finish writing this chapter, and, oh yeah, get some sleep somewhere in there too.

If my goal is to finish writing this chapter, but I go start a load of laundry and decide to sweep the dog fur off my hallway floor, I'm putting in effort, but I'm not putting in effort on the 'right' thing. Sure, I'll end up with a clean house and feel happier about that, but I'll miss the mark on achieving the goal of finishing writing this chapter. By being clear about what it is that we're working on achieving, the effort we put in starts to become much more specific.

Being specific about where you focus your effort and energy is incredibly helpful in maximizing the results you get, because your time spent in training the skills you need for achieving a goal will be far more efficient. Ever heard of the 80/20 rule? While we've come to call it the 80/20 rule, this rule was originally known as the Pareto Principle. This principle, originally developed by Italian economist Vilfredo Pareto in 1896, states that 80% of consequences or outcomes come from 20% of causes or efforts.

It's easy to misinterpret this principle and say that you can minimize your effort down to 20% and still achieve 80% of what you want. No, no, no, mon ami. It's not about the amount of effort you're putting in; it's about being ultra-specific in how you *focus* your effort so that you get what you want. This is all about helping you identify which tasks to prioritize in order to get the most bang for your buck.

So. Here we are, with an ultra-dissected, microscopic breakdown of what to consider and keep in perspective in the process of training. On one side of training, there's how to think about and decide on the amount of effort you put into achieving goals so you become more efficient in the process of training. On the other side of training, there's staying aware of what snags you can hit along the way and how to manage those little buggers. Both sides count, and need your attention throughout the process of training.

It's easy to get caught up in the minutia of it all, so if you're feeling a wee bit overwhelmed, please just start with this:

- KISS - Keep it simple, silly.
- Be specific.
- Take it one step at a time.
- Focus on getting savagely good at the boring and basic, because that's where you're going to start to level up. Boring and basic are way more important than you think they are; they're the foundation – and strong foundations matter.

By focusing on building consistency with the simple things, this is how you become who you most desire to be. You can add in the minutia and the details over time.

The habits you develop through the process of training consistently on the skills of building a growth mindset, being more resilient, knowing who you are, and living in alignment with your values, are the pathway to living boldly, on the terms you create for yourself.

As James Clear said in his book 'Atomic Habits':

'Making a choice that is 1% better or 1% worse is insignificant in the moment. But over the span of moments that make up a lifetime, these choices determine the difference between who you are and who you could be.'

— JAMES CLEAR

I can't think of a better reason to train than to go and chase down the possibility of who you can become, so that you can write your own playbook, act according to your own set of rules, and live the life of your dreams.

TRAINING JOURNAL PROMPT

Identify one area of your life that you've been dreaming about improving. Take that dream, write that sucker out in the form of a SMART goal, and make a plan for it. What skills or behaviors will you need to train so you can achieve that goal? Include your feelings about the goal (such as if the goal makes you anxious, and what you'll do to manage that anxiety) in your plan. Remember, if you fail to plan, you plan to fail.

A RECAP OF GRIIT

Growth

A growth mindset is the foundation for living well and practicing self-leadership. A growth mindset means you believe in your ability to continue to learn new things and embrace challenges while on the way to becoming the person you were always meant to be.

Resilience

Being resilient means feeling confident and competent in your ability to do hard things. Building competence happens by being courageous, brave, and being willing to take a risk. The more your risks work out, the more confident you'll be in yourself.

Identity

Your identity is not what you do; it's who you are. This is the collection of strengths and weaknesses, hopes and fears, wants and needs, boundaries, expectations, quirks, characteristics, and more, which make you, you.

Integrity

Leading with integrity means you are taking responsibility for your choices and actions. Your values system is the thing that shapes your moral compass, informs your purpose in the world, and keeps you humble enough to always want to continue to learn.

Training

All skills are perishable if they are not consistently trained on. Take the skills from each of the previous pillars of GRIIT, and make a plan for how you will consistently train them. And remember, effort counts.

PART II

POWER

'Happiness isn't the absence of problems, but the ability to deal with them.'

— STEVE MARABOLI, 'LIFE, THE TRUTH, AND BEING FREE'

Life is beautiful, but it's also a four-letter word. And, as much as I'm clearly a fan of using well-placed expletives as sentence enhancers and adjectives, it's not the greatest experience when life turns from being sweet, to... well, sour.

It's inevitable that any and all of us will be faced with problems at various points in life, no matter how skilled we are at living well. Problems are, simply put, a part of life. What we choose to do with those problems, though, is key. The simple fact that you're here, reading this book, taking in this information, says to me that you want to live well, and to do so on your own terms. Part of living well means recognizing the power you have in being able to choose, autonomously, how to solve problems in a way that lines up with who you are, what you value, and the direction you want to continue to move your life in.

One of the most important parts of living well is recognizing the power you have in being a fully autonomous being. Now wait: *autonomous*... there's a $50 word, eh? Let's talk about what that means.

Having autonomy means you get to make a judgment call on something without being pressured into a decision by someone or something else. In other words, it's getting to stand on your own two feet and decide how you want to handle your shit without someone else telling you what to do or how to do it.

So, you get to choose. You get to make the call on whether you want to address something, avoid the hell out of it, or ask someone else to do the work for you. You. Get. To. Choose. But, with every choice you make, it's necessary to remember you are never, ever free of the consequence of that choice. The funky thing about consequences is that we're taught to think of consequence as the 'Big Bad'. Sure, that can be a possible outcome – but what if you choose to take the chance of applying for your dream job, and then you LAND IT?! Getting that dream job is as much a consequence of the choice to apply, as it would be to not get it as a result of choosing to not apply, because you were too scared to risk the possibility of getting turned down. You miss 100% of the shots you don't take.

Consequences are simply the result of an action. Sometimes they're sexy, sweet, and everything we could only imagine in our wildest dreams, and then there's times they're about as fun as stepping on a LEGO piece. (Or a Barbie shoe. Lemme tell you what *that* feels like as you're blindly searching your way down the hall, in the dark, for a midnight loo break and trying not to wake up your tiny human...)

Addressing the problems we inevitably will face throughout life involves first making the choice to be willing to address it at all. Being willing to address a problem is all about staying open to the possibility of a better outcome, but if you avoid addressing it, you're no better than the screaming toddler being carried like a surfboard out of Target after his mama decided she had enough and hit 'abandon cart' in her head. The willful stuff isn't going to work if you want to live boldly and well. Stay open, stay willing.

Dr. Benjamin Hardy, an organizational psychologist, said this about problems:

> 'Small things, if not corrected, become big things, always.'
>
> — DR. BENJAMIN HARDY

I've found over and over again, that people avoid addressing problems because they actually have no idea where to begin. Facing problems and figuring out how to deal with them in the process of trying to course correct can be a legitimately overwhelming experience, and it's valid if you want to skip town each time an issue pops up. That said, skipping town is only going to keep that self-sabotage cycle going that you've been stuck in. This is where POWER comes in.

POWER is all about helping you stop letting sabotage creep in (like the creeper it is) and mess with the relationship you have with yourself and the world around you each time a problem gets dropped in your lap. You deserve to feel good about yourself and confident in your ability to handle things when life turns into a four-letter word, don't you think?

For POWER to be effective, it needs the strong, proactive foundation of GRIIT, especially when it comes to having a growth mindset and being resilient. But POWER is reactive – after all, needing POWER comes up when something's happened that now has to be dealt with.

POWER stands for:

Pause for Perspective
Observe and Organize
Work the Problem
Express the Impact
Recover

Remember, problems are a normal, inevitable part of life. They're just speedbumps. To live well, you need a better way of getting past those speedbumps strategically and safely, instead of pulling a 'Dukes of Hazzard' and launching yourself into oblivion. POWER is the problem-solving strategy you never knew you always needed. <*You're welcome.*>

Let's get into it, shall we?

6

PAUSE FOR PERSPECTIVE

> 'The inspiration you seek is already within you. Be silent and listen.'
>
> — RUMI

One of my most favorite words is *Interoception*.

It sounds ridiculous when you're trying to figure out how to say it, so it's a sure hit for a giggle or three, and it's so science-y that you're sure to feel like a whole entire smart person if you can figure out how to fit it into an actual sentence. I double-dog dare you to try.

I first heard this word when I was buried in a nutrition coaching certification I decided to take (because I live that 'Forever Student' life), and my inner nerd instantly geeked out and wanted to know more. The more I learned about interoception, the more I realized that not only is this one of the most important things we need to solve problems well; it also gets stronger the more often we check in with it.

So, let's define it.

Interoception is actually one of our senses - you know, like sight and sound – but we're not taught to think of it as a sense. (Which is dumb. I'm telling you that it's one of the senses, and you totally have my permission to joke around with people that you have a sixth sense and watch them freak out. You're welcome!) Interoception helps us both feel what's going on inside our bodies, while making sense of those feelings at the same time. If you've ever felt your heart racing before the start of something you've been practicing for, like a 5k race, a theater show you're in the cast of, or a big test, you probably associate that racing heart with a bit of anxiety. Similarly, if you've accomplished a really big goal that you weren't sure you could actually reach, and you're celebrating in the heat of the moment with friends, you probably also felt your heart racing and associated it with joy and excitement, instead of anxiety. Just like metacognition is thinking about our thinking, interoception is thinking about and feeling our feelings.

Interoception helps a ton with things like staying emotionally cool as a cucumber instead of turning into a lit fuse, but it also helps us be motivated to do things. If you feel goosebumps on your arms, you're going to identify that feeling as being chilly and go grab a sweater. Or if your stomach is grumbling, you'll go grab a snacky-snack. The motivation for behaviors absolutely comes from interoception, just as much as emotional self-regulation also comes from it.

So why does this matter when it comes to problem-solving? One, because you need to pause to get perspective and feel the feelings (interoception), and two, because you (and I, and all the people roaming this space ball we call home) have a fun little thing called the 'limbic system'. For the sake of not turning this into a whole-ass science lesson, let's just say the limbic system is the part of the brain that helps us stay alive. It's the built-in 'oh shit' button that helps us not only scan for danger, but react to it when life happens to drop a big ole' problem-o in our lap. The limbic system does a really important job for us, but it also can seriously mess with our interoception in a couple instances.

One is neurodiversity, and the other is trauma. Although they happen in different ways, neurodiversity and trauma both affect the way we interpret the signals our body is sending to us. For many people with different types of neurodiversity, it's very common to struggle with identifying body signals such as hunger, having difficulty with naming emotions, or, on the flip side, feeling very confident in being able to name what they physically and emotionally feel but having their experience questioned or mislabeled by people around them. This can send their limbic system into overdrive because, all of a sudden, the world around them no longer feels safe. It's hella hard to be neurodiverse in a world that's set up for neurotypical people.

Just the same as neurodiverse people struggle with interoception, so can people who have lived through trauma. When a person is in the middle of a traumatic experience, the limbic system lights up and goes to work to keep that person alive, both literally and figuratively. *But* the limbic system needs to 'turn off' again once the traumatic experience is over. Sometimes, our brains forget how to turn that switch back off, and the limbic system stays activated well after a traumatic event is over. This is a large part of why people often describe feeling like they're not 'the same' again after going through some seriously shitty things. They can logically realize they're not being threatened by trauma anymore, but their body is stuck in 'fight-flight-freeze' mode.

To problem-solve at all, let alone do it well, you have to first be able to turn the limbic system's 'switch' off to get back in tune with your interoception sense. This is why the first step to really nailing this whole problem-solving thing is just simply hitting the pause button so that you can get some perspective on what you feel and why you're feeling it.

Now let's be clear here for a hot second, the problems we're going to talk about throughout POWER are <u>NOT</u> life or death problems. I hope to dear, sweet baby Jesus you're not ever in that kind of situation, but dealing with a life-or-death problem is a *very* different kind of thing, and needs to be dealt with in a different way than what we're getting into here. We're talking about the problems any of us could fall over in the course of typical life, things like: kids being jerks to their parents, divorce or the ending of another type of important relationship, burnout at work, being overwhelmed with moving to a new home, financial issues, etc. These things can be legitimately big issues to deal with, but they are not life-or-death issues.

Now that we've got that out of the way, I bet you're thinking:

'Kelly, this sounds really complicated. How can I pause when things feel so serious and heavy?'

The first thing to remember is, more often than not, the things which feel the most complicated and heavy usually require the simplest answers. We tend to complicate the fuck out of things because we're taught that big, complicated problems require big, complicated answers and solutions, *right now*, with absolutely all the urgency we can muster instantaneously. Nay, friend, nay. Why make life harder than it already feels?

When I was a kid, I remember being the one in my family who was always stuck in my head. I was emotional, got easily lost in my thoughts, and generally didn't want to talk about my very big feelings. But I also wore my heart on my sleeve (still do), and one look at my face could tell you exactly what I was feeling. My dad could always read me. In our family, he and I are the most alike, so metric tons of words weren't really necessary. He'd see my face, know the gist of what was up, and would intervene so my mom wouldn't have to. In those moments, he'd say to me:

'Kel, simple is more better. Just keep it simple.'

My dad and I have always been close. He had this way of getting my wild heart in check quickly and easily, and with very few words imparted in the process (usually said with a handful of intentional grammatical inaccuracies for the sake of making a funny). This was a lesson that had to be reinforced to me over and over again through my teen and young adult years, but it finally sunk in. Over time, I realized the importance of not only having simple answers to the complicated fuckery life can throw at us, but in having strategies we can use as we work through problems step by step, because those strategies give us a bigger feeling of being in control when everything else feels chaotic. Simply put: Simple + Strategic = Successful Problem-Solving.

In the moments of my dad reminding me that 'simple is more better', he was reminding me to pause and get perspective before moving forward. Remember, if your limbic system is all lit up on high alert, there's a lot of perspective that gets lost.

When you hit the pause button, you have to make good use of that time. It's not a moment to go kick back and do nothing – this is a pause on problem-solving, but is still a time for you to be very active. Making good use of a pause when you recognize your limbic system is freaking out means you're actively engaging in grounding exercises, in order to come down from the stratosphere and chill out a bit before moving forward again. The more you get your nervous system to be cool, calm, and collected, the more you'll be able to get back in touch with your interoceptive (my fave word!!) sense. Then, you can use it as another tool to problem-solve effectively.

Now I know talking about 'oh, go do this grounding exercise and everything will be fine' probably sounds like some hippie-dippie stuff – I promise you it's not (even though the hippie-dippie stuff is a personal favorite of yours truly!). Grounding exercises are backed by a whole lot of science, and are a way to calm your nervous system down, get emotionally squared away, and stay connected to the present moment. It's so ridiculously easy for our brains to start doing some really squirrely shit when we get freaked out by things, so we need a way to get back in check with reality. Grounding is the way we do that.

Examples of grounding exercises include:

- Practicing mindfulness by working on being aware of what you feel and why you feel it
- Meditating
- Going for a walk or a run
- Using your senses by naming five things you can see, four things you can touch, three things you can hear, two things you can smell, and one thing you can taste
- Using positive words and phrases, such as 'calm' or 'I can handle this'
- Making a list of items around you that make you feel safe
- Practicing deep breathing
- Holding an ice cube in your hand or trace it along your forearm, focusing on the sensation of the cold
- Standing on the floor with bare feet, and focus on the feeling of your feet being stable underneath you
- Taking a shower or a bath
- Snuggling your pet
- Counting backwards from 100 by increments of seven
- Coloring
- Getting into the gym for a heavy weight lifting session
- Listening to music
- Journaling about what you're feeling

I promise you, even if it doesn't feel like it, there *is* time to take care of yourself before you jump into problem-solving mode, and you're going to be more effective in tackling things when you've taken the time to get yourself all the way together. It's so easy to get caught up in the urgency of the moment and feel like you have to do everything instantly, when really, you don't. Remember, we're not talking about life-or-death situations here. We're talking about life, life problems, and how to handle them successfully.

Take the time.

Pause for perspective.

Then proceed. You'll thank me later.

PERSPECTIVE JOURNAL PROMPT

Make a list of ten grounding exercises you want to experiment with. These can be things you currently do, and they can also be things you've never done before or haven't done in a long time. Once you've got your list, start trying them! Notice how they make you feel: do you feel calmer, more anxious, or the same as you felt when you started the exercise? What did you like about the exercises? What did you dislike? Was there anything you felt indifferent towards? Write those observations down and keep trying different ways to ground until you have a list of ten exercises you find effective.

7

OBSERVE AND ORGANIZE

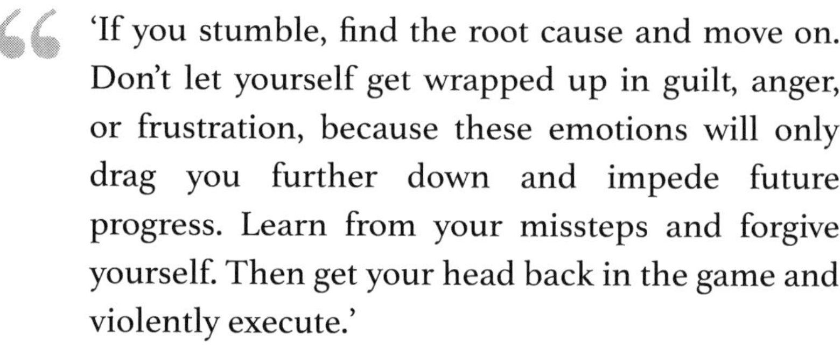

I'll never forget the moment it happened.

When I was going to school to learn how to be an EMT, the instructors warned us of what would happen if my classmates or I got too overwhelmed emotionally on a chaotic scene. Over and over again, they told us stories of their partners getting overwhelmed and freezing up; stories of personally experiencing freezing up; the ways they all got themselves in check so they could continue doing their jobs.

When a person freezes, it's because they've hit a point of emotional saturation where they literally can't process what's happening around them anymore, along with being unable to make themselves react to their environment. It's the 1000-yard stare, happening in technicolor either to you, or right in front of you.

I was in my very early 20s, working for an EMS company in a major Connecticut city, known for its gang violence. Working New Year's Eve in this city was a crapshoot – it was either going to be a night where we sat around waiting for someone to call 911, or we would be running back-to-back emergencies all night. This particular New Year's Eve, I was overtired from working double shifts while also going to school for my bachelor's degree and dealing with internships, I was stressed from arguing with my then-boyfriend, and while I normally tolerated it pretty well, I was especially irritated by the level of debauchery happening that night in the city. Between the shootings, stabbings, overdoses, and other calls that didn't need 911, I was at my limit. The fatigue, stress, and irritation I was feeling was the trifecta of 'this isn't going to end well'.

My partner and I responded to a car crash around 2am, and the city was showing no signs of slowing down for the night. All my partner and I wanted was for the city residents to *just go to freaking bed already*. But here we were, at 2am, running yet another call. I was lucky to be working that shift with an experienced, multi-decade paramedic, who was tired but otherwise unbothered by the ridiculousness of the night.

We pulled up to the scene of a single car crash – the driver had plowed straight into a light pole, knocking it over and dumping the liquid contents of his engine all over the street. With antifreeze and oil everywhere, we had to call for the fire department to come clean it up, while the single police officer that was with us stood watch as we went to work taking care of the driver (who was so deeply under the influence that he was feeling '*fine*', despite having just totaled his car. As we were in the process of starting to care for the driver and waiting (not so patiently) for the fire department to get on scene, we heard gunfire that, by the sound of it, was roughly two or so blocks away. Far too close for comfort. This wasn't the first time I had been on an emergency call and had gunfire happening close by – that was actually a relatively normal occurrence for this city. But it was the first time I completely, utterly froze.

Between being as tired, stressed, and irritated as I was, I didn't have any brain space left to emotionally or logically process more information. It's like a kitchen sponge being run under water, starting when it's completely bone dry. It's going to absorb quite a bit at first, it'll expand so that it's usable, and then – and it happens faster than you think it will - it's suddenly full and overflowing. I was an overflowing sponge. Too much information being thrown at me with not enough space to take it all in. My nervous system was about as much of a wreck as our patient's car.

I heard the gunfire, stood straight up and looked at my partner; he said 'we need to leave quickly', and I commenced to do... *nothing*. I heard the words come out of his mouth, recognized his statement as being very accurate, and then I just stopped. I was totally frozen and completely checked out of what was going on around me. (For first responders, this is a very dangerous situation.) My partner came around to the side of the car I was standing on, yelled in my face (which did exactly nada to wake me back up), and when that didn't work, he put his hands on my shoulders and gave me a solid shove. To be clear, this guy was one of the nicest, most respectful male partners I ever had. I always felt safe, was watched out for, and was treated incredibly well when working with him. Throwing me physically off balance was the exact thing I ended up needing in that moment in order to pull me back to being aware of my surroundings because it was like a jolt to my very frozen nervous system. I'm so grateful he did exactly that, so we could do our job and get off that scene as fast as possible. Neither one of us wanted to stick around and chance collecting extra holes in our bodies.

I learned an incredible lesson that night: how terrifying it was to be in a position where I froze up like that, and how important it was to learn how to stay aware of the impact my emotions had on me (especially when I'm super-freaking-extra tired), in order to accomplish the task in front of me.

In the quote at the start of this chapter, Brent Gleeson, former member of Seal Team 5, talks about not getting lost in the emotions that kick up when you screw up or something doesn't go your way. Instead, he says you have to forgive yourself, learn the lesson, and get back to work so you can accomplish the task at hand. When you've taken a moment to pause and get some perspective, and you're ready to get back to work, it's important to recognize how much problem-solving has to become tactical. You're out there, working your ass off to accomplish a purpose, and if you let your emotions take over like I did when I froze, you're going to get thrown off course 100% of the time.

But that doesn't mean your emotions don't matter or have a place in the process of problem-solving. Problem-solving doesn't work when it's emotionally *driven* – but it tends to work very well when it's emotionally *informed*.

If you're throwing yourself forward, trying to figure out a problem, but letting your emotions run amuck like a group of unchecked teens wandering the floors of the local mall, you're not going to get very far. You're going to catch yourself being impulsive, probably making some poor choices, and getting caught up in emotional misfires that just cause more damage than they're worth. This is what it means to be *reactive* to a situation - it's fast, very emotional, impulsive, and not usually very well thought out. On the flip side, when you're moving forward with intention and purpose (because you paused first to get your head screwed back on straight), you still acknowledge your emotions, but instead use them as check points for not just *why* you want to move forward, but *how* you want to move forward. This is all about being *responsive* instead of reactive. Being responsive to a situation means you're moving a little bit slower – you're taking the time to think and consider before you do anything (observing), and your choices will tend to be less emotional and more rational (organizing).

The first real step in being able to move forward deliberately and decisively with problem-solving is to observe the problem by learning how to practice situational awareness. This idea is a person's ability to stay aware of what's happening or changing in their environment, and how those changes can affect both their present and future. If you're walking down the sidewalk with your face buried in your phone because Mr. Cute Guy (or Girl) from the next cubicle over finally decided to text you, you're not going to notice the out-of-control car barreling towards you. In that instance, you're allowing your emotions to drive your decision-making, leaving you buried in your phone because you're caught up in the moment. Instead, if you were emotionally informed, you would choose to allow yourself to feel excited about wanting to text Cute Guy/Girl back (because let's be real, this *is* exciting!), but put your phone in your pocket and keep your head up to watch your surroundings as you walk to the coffee shop down the street. Once you stroll through the coffee shop door, then and only then will you text them back, because you're an intelligent, grown-ass adult who knows what's up when it comes to safety, problem-solving, and managing your surroundings. The more emotionally informed you practice being, the more you're going to also practice situational awareness.

Situational awareness allows you to take in information from your environment, because you're constantly practicing observing what's happening around you. When you keep your head up and just simply take the time to notice what's going on inside you (your emotions... remember interoception!) in relation to what's going on around you (your relationships and environment), you'll put yourself in a better position to be able to decide with actual clarity what is and is not important at any given moment. The more time you allow yourself to just simply observe, the more you'll be surprised by how much you let matter in the past that really didn't matter all that much. Taking the time to observe helps us be more efficient in figuring out what things actually need to be focused on and prioritized.

Two things to be aware of in the process of practicing observing are your biases and dialectics. Way back in the chapter about Growth, we talked about dialectics – this is the fun little idea that two opposing things can be true at the same time. (What can I say... it keeps things spicy.) When you're taking the time to observe what you're feeling in relation to what's happening around you, it's entirely possible to start feeling like you're gaslighting yourself because things just aren't lining up the way you want them to. Problems don't tend to show up wrapped in neat, tidy boxes with pretty little bows on top, so chances are fairly good that you're not gaslighting yourself; you're just dealing with opposite things happening at the same time.

Let's say you're now in a relationship with Mr. Cute Guy (or Girl) from the next cubicle over. You've been dating for a year, and as you've gotten to know each other at deeper levels, you realize that you're now in a relationship with one of the most intelligent people you've ever known. But they're also clueless when it comes to 'reading the room' and recognizing when they're not meeting your emotional needs. (Love languages, anyone?) So, you have a problem. You practice observing, recognizing that while you care deeply for this person, they're the emotional equivalent of an awkward pre-teen when it comes to social awareness and being a supportive partner. The 'opposites' in this situation can be crazy-making, because it leaves people questioning themselves and what they feel, when really, the opposites of being intelligent while lacking self-awareness are valid, real things that happen, but also create the problem of an emotionally disconnected relationship.

If you spent time in other relationships feeling devalued, ignored, or with your needs not being met, you could have a bias against people who lack self-awareness because you realize how crazy-making it is for you to be around that. Yet you didn't realize this about Mr. Cute Guy/Miss Cute Girl until you were already in too deep and caught some pretty big feelings for them. <Yikes> You continue to practice observing, realizing you're feeling anxious and sad about the situation, while also feeling scared of losing the relationship because you're invested and do have real feelings. At the same time, you notice yourself being angry at having yet another experience of feeling like you're being discarded by someone you care for. So the opposites that are happening (your partner being intelligent while also lacking self-awareness), combined with your bias against people who lack self-awareness, just upped the ante on the problem you're now aware of.

And that's where we need to organize. Once you've spent time observing – whether it's moments or months – the next step in problem-solving is figuring out what pieces of information you want to prioritize, and in what order you want to prioritize them in. This means that you're now making decisions about which parts of a problem have to be dealt with first, versus which parts can wait a bit, versus which parts actually don't matter at all.

In your relationship with Mr. Cute Guy/Miss Cute Girl, you realize you want to do what's realistically possible to preserve the relationship, but that you also don't want to compromise on your need to feel emotionally fulfilled by it. You decide that the priorities you want to address in a conversation about this problem are how your partner's lack of awareness affects you emotionally, and that you want to make it clear to them that you don't want to spend your time being anxious, sad, and angry about history repeating itself. In this example, you used observation to be aware of your emotions first. Then, that awareness was used to inform (but not control) how you organized your thought process about prioritizing the things you want to deal with so you can successfully solve this problem.

Just like pausing for perspective requires you to slow way down, so does observing and organizing. To solve problems efficiently and effectively, it's important to make sure you're fully aware of yourself and your emotions about a problem (pausing for perspective). Then you can see the bigger picture (observing) and decide what matters to you (organizing) in the process of addressing the problem. If you're moving at warp speed, you're going to miss the details that matter.

Once you're there, then it's time to work out the problem and wrangle that sucker into submission.

OBSERVE AND ORGANIZE JOURNAL PROMPT

Take some time to notice whether or not you've ever consciously chosen to slow down to practice observing and organizing before addressing a problem. If you've just plowed ahead, how has that gone for you? How do you think slowing down to practice observing and organizing information first, before problem solving, would affect you?

8

WORK THE PROBLEM

'We cannot solve our problems with the same level of thinking that created them.'

— ALBERT EINSTEIN

Sometimes, things are complicated. But they often don't need to be – they become complicated because we make solving problems so much harder than they have to be.

I like being part of a team. It's exciting, being able to work towards a common goal with someone, and when you also like that person or group of people, it happens to be a lot of fun (most of the time). I've had the privilege of being part of a hell of a lot of really cool teams; there's something about teamwork that's just *neat*.

That good feeling is a fun little thing called *collective effervescence*: it's a feeling of energy and harmony people get when they're all working together towards a common goal. When the team gels really well, that effervescent feeling builds up even more. That harmonious feeling makes working on problems easier because working with people you like, while also feeling supported and offering support right back simultaneously, is incredibly rewarding and motivating.

But what happens if it doesn't work, or if you're on your own?

Pull up a chair. Let me tell you about the worst supervisor I've ever had.

I had been working for a public community mental health agency for a few years, and the turnover rate for supervisory staff was crazy high. In two and a half years of being there, I watched no less than six different supervisors come and go. Some moved up in the company; others just simply moved on. The final supervisor I had prior to my own departure was... not spectacular.

As it often happens in public agencies, she was a political hire from another division in the company, because she was known for doing what management told her to do. Upper management wanted to fill the open spot with a 'yes man', and she was it. The team I worked with had been together for several years, and we were tight. This was the kind of team where we all had open-door policies with each other, we were constantly caught hanging out in each other's offices, and if you needed help with something, all you had to do was find an open door and start talking. It was fantastic. The outgoing supervisor was leaving for the Peace Corps and was well-liked, so the team was also feeling the loss. We always had two supervisors that shared the responsibility of supervising the team, and each one managed half of us.

When the new supervisor came in, we were all guarded, not just because she was the 'new kid', but because none of us had heard great things about her. We were protective of each other and didn't want to lose what we had.

Quickly, the new supervisor let us all know exactly where we stood with her. There was no 'team' – there was her, and then the rest of us. It was crystal clear that we were to do as we were told, and if we had a problem with something, we either had to deal with it, or present a solution she deemed acceptable, instead of being able to brainstorm alongside her. It sucked. Team morale quickly dropped, and for the therapists who were assigned to her, managing client caseloads became extraordinarily difficult.

In the process of being supervised by her, she was often inaccessible, sitting in her office most of the time, with the door being left closed as a clear signal she was not to be bothered. Most of the team felt she was unwilling to have conversations; rather, she wanted to talk 'at' us and then send us away again. I felt like she was the exact opposite of someone I could rely on and look up to.

The resolutions she'd present to the team during meetings, for problems we'd been trying to work through together, were typically far more complex and complicated than they needed to be, and we often felt like we were, frankly, on our own. Instead of working smarter, we just worked harder. It made zero sense.

The bubbling, lively, sweet collective effervescence the team had before her had gone completely flat. Because of the power dynamic she had set up, we all also felt powerless to even try to fix it, no matter how much we understood the situation.

When you're on your own trying to work out a problem, it can feel just as flat as this supervisor left me and my teammates feeling. Being stuck in your head, overthinking, not being sure where to start, and feeling like everything has to be important all at the same time – it's as heavy an impact as my terrible, horrible, no-good, very bad supervisor. (Bonus points to any parents who catch that reference!)

Whether you're on your own working out a problem, or on a team that's struggling, it's possible to get back to that place of fun and ease that collective effervescence creates, but you have to be really intentional in what you're choosing to do and why you're choosing to do it.

In order to actually be effective when working out a problem, it's helpful to think about it in a streamlined way. Let's lay this out in steps. First, go back to pausing and get your nervous system back under control. Then, zoom out on the problem, figure out which parts of the problem actually matter, and put those parts in order of importance. (Pause for perspective, then observe and organize.) Once you've taken care of those steps, move on. You're going to work out the problem either to the point of resolution, or to the point of it being managed if it can't be resolved completely.

The steps here are:

Simplify with specificity
Control the controllables
Use a decision tree

First thing's first, let's define and discuss each point and what to be aware of, and then once we've done that, I'll throw an example your way of what this can all look like strung together.

1. **Simplify with specificity**.

The first and most important step in working out a problem successfully is to just make things simpler. But be *specific* about how you're actually choosing to simplify it. People typically think on a spectrum ranging from super complicated to overly simplified. At one end of that spectrum is an idea called '*complexity bias*', which is a fun little thing that says the more complicated something is, the better. It builds up this idea that if human beings naturally think something seems too simple or obvious, it's too good to be true and it's supposed to be more complicated. So off we go, looking for the more complicated solutions to solve all the world's problems with, instead of looking at the simple thing that happens to be right at our feet, just waiting for us to pick it up. Because we're geared up to look for the more complicated solutions or answers to problems, this also leads a lot of people to really get trapped in avoidance. Remember, the more complicated something feels, the more overwhelming it's also going to feel, and once that happens, it's way too easy to get caught up in all the feely-feelings and never do anything at all. Eff that.

At the other end of this spectrum is an idea called '*simplicity bias*'. This idea says that the more obvious and simple an answer seems to be, the better. Some people are geared towards simplicity bias, thinking that if they just find *that* thing – you know, the singular thing that will fix all their issues – everything will be right and well in the world again. Not so, friend.

We need to simplify issues in order to work on resolving them for sure. But we also need to keep in perspective that simplicity bias and complexity bias are the two extremes of a spectrum, and our job is to land somewhere in the middle. Remember, when anything is taken to an extreme, it automatically becomes unhelpful or unhealthy. Don't make things overly complicated, but don't oversimplify them either. Problem-solving needs to be more simplified than not, but just because we make it simple, this doesn't necessarily mean it's always going to be easy. Simple and easy are two very different things. There can be extremely important, but also complex, details that have to be taken into account in the process of problem-solving, so the best thing any of us can do in the process of simplifying is balancing out asking very specific, valuable questions with keeping an open mind and allowing for a combination of different things to come together as the 'best, right' answer.

To simplify properly and effectively, focus on asking questions that are highly specific and based on what will bring value to the process of solving the specific problem you're working on. Any high-value, specific question you can ask will bring significant value to the process of problem-solving. It puts guardrails around the whole shebang, keeping you on track and in your lane while reducing all the other irrelevant crap you could potentially get caught up in.

2. <u>Control the controllables.</u>

Once we've taken the time to work on simplifying by asking better questions, the next step is to 'control the controllables'. I say this to people all the time because it is *that* important. When we focus our attention on the big picture of the whole problem, it's too easy to get caught up in the chaos of it all. By getting specific and asking those better questions about what's realistic to do in that particular situation or circumstance, the things that truly can be controlled will start to reveal themselves.

Throughout each pillar of POWER, controlling the controllables shows up from controlling our nervous system, to managing our perspective and what we choose to focus on, to taking control over the chaos of a problem by coming up with strategies for management or resolution – this is a theme that's important to pay attention to. Any time we're faced with a problem, there's always going to be a level of chaos that's involved. When we slow down, focus on what's actionable and where the possibility for impact exists, and then direct our efforts there, problems, all of a sudden, start to become a lot smaller and much more manageable.

So take the 'controllables' one step at a time; get those out of the way. Once you've handled those, the parts of problem-solving that are left over are the unknowns. These are the factors in problems that no one – unless you're psychic – can plan for or predict, so don't overthink it, or you'll run the risk of creating problems that haven't happened yet. The unknowns have to be dealt with as they occur, from deciding whether or not you need to deal with it right away, if it can wait or if it matters at all, to deciding what you want to do about it, and then taking action on it.

The unknown will always be a factor when it comes to problem-solving, and that's ok. It's just something to be aware of and prepare for – if or when it happens.

3. Climb a tree – a decision tree!

From there, the final step of working the problem is to use 'decision trees' to organize yourself around what you're wanting the outcome of your problem to be, and the different options you have in getting to that outcome. Decision trees are a great way to organize a thought process when a problem is really rocking your world, because they're specifically designed to organize problems and data into simple, easy-to-understand paths. Let's break that down a bit:

Decision trees get your thought process organized by creating a visual for it as you're working on different strategies and solutions for problems. They're made up of:

Root: the problem you're trying to solve or manage.
Decision: this contains information about the decision you're trying to make.
Chances: this contains details about the possible unknowns or things that can't be controlled immediately.

Alternatives: possible outcomes, action steps to take, or things that could still happen with this problem.
Rejected alternatives: branches that show a possible choice that you decided to bail on. It's helpful to leave these on your decision tree because they add context to your thought process. Remember, be specific.
Endpoints: this is the solution or management strategy you end up choosing and has more information about the final outcome of the problem.

Let's go back to the problem of my terrible, no-good, very bad supervisor and use that as an example to make this make more sense. (Did you catch that reference yet?!)

First thing's first: simplify with specificity. To face the problem of how we'd work successfully with her, my team and I first had to figure out how to get really specific about this problem, without complicating it. We knew we needed to simplify and get focused on what we were truly mad about, otherwise, we'd end up just being a bunch of Petty Bettys and going to upper management, which would only have made the issue worse. So, we started by making a list of what we wanted to be angry at, and then we eliminated the unhelpful (and sometimes ridiculous) items by asking specific questions. Here's an example of a helpful question we asked: 'Are we angry about tangible things, such as changes to our paperwork requirements? Or are we angry about intangible things, such as feeling like we can't control what happened to our team, along with being angry that our supervisor isn't interested in getting to know us or understanding the needs of our team?'. Once we realized we were angry about the intangible things, we were able to continue to get more specific from there.

It's important here to remember that there are good questions – those are the ones that help you get specific, and there are not-so-good, unhelpful questions to ask. They're unhelpful because they just get you more stuck. One unhelpful question a team member asked, as we were working together on figuring out what we were upset about, was about which parts of the supervisor's personality we most disliked. This just led to gossip, bigger emotions, and resistance to wanting to address the issue. Don't let the unhelpful questions get you more wrapped up in a problem – identify them, eliminate them from your question list, and move on.

Now onto step two. Once we simplified and identified the actual issue, we moved on to controlling the controllables. We realized first that we couldn't control how supervisors were chosen and assigned to different teams, or what our new supervisor's personality was like. Focusing on those things wouldn't have been helpful, so we had to make the conscious choice not to put effort into them because it would have been wasted time and energy. Instead, we focused on what we could control: where our leadership was coming from, how we could communicate with each other and with leadership about the issues with the supervisor, and how we could address liability issues and protect our clients when the supervisor made a clinical choice we disagreed with. We also helped each other make concrete plans for self-care after a difficult day, knowing that we weren't going to get that same kind of support from our supervisor.

Lastly, let's look at how we applied the decision tree. The root of the problem is that she was, well, pretty terrible. The decision my team and I were trying to make was how in the hell we were going to tolerate her. The chances we had to deal with were that her moods were unpredictable, we couldn't control that she provided us with little access to her, and that we never knew when she was going to bail early for the day, leaving us without any leadership – even if it was crappy leadership.

We decided our alternatives were to seek more support from the supervisor for the other half of the team, along with asking for more help from the supervisors of other programs that we regularly worked with. We agreed to have direct conversations with this supervisor about our concerns, and that we also had the option to file complaints to upper management. Eventually, we decided to reject the idea of filing complaints, because we all agreed that wouldn't go anywhere or help our cause.

In discussion, we agreed our endpoint was to begin with having direct conversations with the supervisor about the problems we had with her, and if those conversations didn't produce results, we'd go to the other supervisors we had access to for more help.

Was it perfect? Heck no. Did it help make the problem a little less bad? Absolutely, and that was the goal. This was a situation where there wasn't going to be a real resolution, so the problem had to be managed instead.

See how that works?

Decision trees are a fantastic way to break your thought process down about the options and alternatives that you have at your fingertips when it comes to working out a problem.

Your job, in working out the problem, is to:

1. Keep your thought process somewhere in between overly simple and overly complicated
2. Control the controllables
3. Use a decision tree to work through your options, to figure out what's going to make the most sense and be the most useful.

This kind of organizing, under these three points, is a great tool you can come back to over and over again. Rework it and redo it as much as you need to, and use it to keep yourself organized, focused, and go get control over the problems you face one by one. It's both helpful and necessary to have tools and strategies like this to rely on when you're dealing with a problem that feels overwhelming or bigger than you know what to do with. Just like simplifying a problem by being specific acts as a set of guardrails for your thought process, this does, too.

Now that you've got problem-solving down to a science – it's time to take care of you.

WORK THE PROBLEM JOURNAL PROMPT

Name a problem you've been avoiding dealing with. Simplify it by getting specific about the issue, and list out what you can realistically control in that situation. Then, build a decision tree around how to either manage the problem, or resolve it completely. What's the strategy for management/resolution you have come up with? How do you feel about that strategy?

9

EXPRESS THE IMPACT

> ‘There are thousands of causes for stress, and one antidote to stress is self-expression. That’s what happens to me every day. My thoughts get off my chest, down my sleeves, and onto my pad.’
>
> — GARSON KANIN

We’re all going to experience the emotional parts of problem-solving in different ways. Some of us will find it entirely exhausting, feeling totally overwhelmed in the process and run down after the fact, while others will be excited at the prospect of attacking a challenge, figuring out how to overcome it and celebrating when victory is achieved.

No matter how you personally experience problem-solving, it’s going to have an impact on you and your nervous system – there’s no way around that. The act of addressing a problem creates a stress response that’s incredibly normal and natural for all of us, regardless of whether we look at it as exciting or exhausting. That stress response is a physical reaction to a 'thing' that's happening in our relationships or environments. It means our bodies will naturally produce stress hormones that help us swing into action to address a problem, but it's important to also stop that stress response when it isn't needed anymore.

The first step in stopping that stress response is just to talk about the impact problems have on your life, and talk about what it's like for you to work on solving or managing problems. Holding everything inside; never talking about how you feel about the problems you've faced; telling everyone 'I'm good' – it's like filling a pressure cooker to max capacity, turning the fire on under it, and walking away without setting the relief valve. If you do that, you just made a slow-moving bomb. That cooker is going to explode, and the shrapnel will leave your kitchen sliced open. If you don't have a relief valve for your stress and other emotions, you'll become that bomb, but the shrapnel will slice open parts of your life. That doesn't sound like a good time, so let's not do that, ok?

Talking about the way we experience problems is important, way more important than we're taught to look at talking as being. When we talk about how we've experienced things in order to genuinely understand the impact those things have had on us, we experience things like connection, community, camaraderie, and continued growth, because of the way problem-solving challenges us to expand. Whether you're talking about a problem with someone else and using it as a vent session, talking through a problem you just solved or managed as part of a team, or working on wrapping your head around the impact of a problem on your own, talking about the impact matters.

The process of 'talking it out' in any capacity or way has this fun little effect, called '*the undoing effect of positive emotions*'. It's this super science-y idea that says positive emotions help undo the ways that negative emotions mess with our nervous systems. Said in a more simple way: positive emotions help us calm down when we've just handled something stressful. When we talk about something, 'get it out', and find connection in the process, either with someone else or feel a deeper connection with ourselves, we feel calmer, happier, and more at peace.

Being able to express the impact that a problem had on you, along with the impact you felt in the process of working through that problem, matters. Giving yourself, your problem-solving partner, and/or your team the time and space to debrief from what in the world you just dealt with not only builds ongoing commitment to continuing to solve problems as they come up, but it builds ownership and accountability to what roles different people have in figuring out how to address problems. If you pay attention carefully here, you'll notice that every single pillar of GRIIT has a role not only in helping you stay the course as you work on solving a problem, but they each have a role in how you take care of yourself once you're done working it out, too. Remember, to solve a problem effectively, you need to have your mindset squared away, be resilient enough to face that problem, remember who you are, check in with your values, and train consistently with consistent effort. It's every pillar of GRIIT.

Some of the most important moments I've had in my own life, both personally and professionally, have come in talking about the problems I've faced, once they're over and done with. Many – nay, most – of those moments have happened either in the front seat of an ambulance, or in therapy.

The front of an ambulance is a sacred space, which is often misunderstood by the general public. It's a space where partners argue with each other, laugh with each other, share ridiculous dad jokes, and tell dumb stories about irrelevant crap no one else would understand but them. It's where 'inside' jokes are born, secrets are shared and then put into the vault of friendship, and where many, many tears are shed. While the conversations I've had in the front of my ambulances with my partners will always remain sacred and secret, they have been some of the most healing, cathartic conversations I've ever had. They were the conversations of 'what the fuck just happened' after a 911 with a poor outcome; they were moments of celebration when we did something really hard and had a good outcome; they were moments of figuring out how to be better teammates when something didn't go as planned. It was where conversations about life lessons happened, where support and listening ears were offered, and ownership and accountability were demanded. In many very real ways, it's where I grew up.

Talking about my personal problems in therapy and how I was dealing with them was often just as cathartic. There's something about being able to say your thoughts out loud, get real-time feedback on them, and let the reality of your problems land – it's *important*. Having a space of being able to take the time you need, on your own terms, to wrap your head around the things that are happening in your life and how you're being affected or already have been affected by them is part of how human beings figure out how to heal, grow, and move forward. No matter what, expressing the impact of the upsides and downsides of life is something we all have to walk through if we want to live well. It's ok if therapy isn't your thing, but that doesn't mean you don't need that outlet of talking as a relief valve. Get creative in looking for where outlets could already be showing up in your life. Maybe you have an outlet in a trusted friend, family member, or even a coworker that you're still getting to know. Those relief valves are surprising little buggers, and sometimes show up where we least expect them.

There are a few ways to start working on communicating well, and it begins with perspective.

In the process of communicating about the impact problems have on your life, it's important to remember that there's a point of acceptance all people hit in the process of working out a problem. There's an acceptance of 'this may be as good as it gets', or 'I truly tried as hard as I could and I kicked ass', or, in some cases, an acceptance of 'I couldn't, because I didn't know how'. No matter what, hitting that acceptance point is a normal and natural part of dealing with problems. But here's the thing:

Acceptance doesn't ever equal approval.

Acceptance is a completely different thing from approval. Acceptance is simply a statement of realizing: 'hey, this thing is a fact that can't be argued with', and figuring out how to sit with that. Approval is the belief we attach to something when we deem it as good or worthy. Totally different than just looking at something as a statement of fact, right? Too often, we're told in these subtle, weird ways that we have to put acceptance and approval at the same level, and that's just not the case. So please know that expressing yourself about the impact a problem has had on you, and your acceptance of that impact as fact, doesn't mean you have to approve of it, like it, or be excited about it. Unless the impact is cool, desired, and you're jazzed about it. Then have at it.

From there, actual communication – like saying real words out loud – and knowing how to do it well, matters. Whether you're working on wrapping your head around the fallout of a nasty problem, or you're chattering away with a friend about the coolest result from handling a problem together and what a kick-ass team you make, communicating clearly, directly, and consistently matters.

The whole 'it's not what you say, it's how you say it' – it's a goofy statement, if we're being honest here. What we say (the words we choose and the order they show up in as we let them loose into the world) and how we say those words (you know, putting the right emPHAsis on the right syLLAble) matter equally, but for different reasons. Being able to string some words together into a grammatically correct sentence doesn't make for good communication. It simply shows you're not a grammar doofus.

Communicating well means understanding the difference between intention and impact, knowing that intention is what we mean and impact is what another person hears and feels as a result of our words. Once we're clear on that, having strategies to pull from for talking about how we've been impacted by a problem is important. First, be clear on why talking about the impact of a problem is important to you and what you're trying to achieve through talking. That's your objective. Then, if you're talking about it with someone else who worked on the problem with you, or you're just having a vent session with a friend, be good to that person. Recognize that they're not your punching bag or dumping grounds – they're a whole entire human being who deserves the same amount of attention, care, and energy that you deserve. And finally, remember to communicate in a way you'd feel proud of, where you can maintain your self-respect. At the end of everything, it's important to make sure you carry yourself in a way that lets you sleep well at night.

I'm putting a whole bunch of steps here and breaking communication down to a semi-microscopic level, but don't overthink this. If those steps feel like they're too much, just do this:

Be curious.

Seriously, I mean it. When communication is approached with a sense of curiosity, it changes the game. It's like an automatic permission to slow down, think a bit about what we're saying and what someone else is saying, and ask questions so we can learn more. Curiosity is a good thing, friend. Let it lead you into wanting to know more about the person you're chatting with, and why they feel the way they do. Just the same, let it also lead you into being more curious about your responses to a problem so that you take your time in explaining yourself, your emotions, and your actions. Let curiosity lead the way.

Now last but certainly not least:

That's a lot of talk about talking... What about when you're flying solo, but still need to 'get it out?'

Being able to express the impact of a problem and going through the process of working that problem matters, regardless of whether you're doing that with another person who was in it with you, or you're doing it on your own. This is just a matter of creativity.

So we're still going to take perspective as the first part of expressing the impact of the problem. Acceptance not equaling approval still applies, whether you're on a team or you're on your own. Stick that perspective in your pocket and carry that with you. Always. Next, we're going to move on to strategies you can put to good use to get your thoughts and feelings out.

Things you can do or try include:

- Journaling
- Poetry writing, and then sharing that poetry during spoken word performances
- Therapy (my personal fave)
- Prayer/confession or other religious ceremonies
- Rituals (this can include spiritual rituals, such as writing messages on rice paper and then burning them)
- Meditation through use of affirmations, mantras, or just sitting in silence to be present with your nervous system

When you're working on expressing the impact of a problem and you're doing it solo, you're going to have to be creative and try different things to figure out what feels like the best, right answer for you. There's no way to screw this part up – you may find things you don't like or don't want to do again, but you also may find things that you really like a ton, but only want to do those things a certain way. There's no 'wrong' answer; there's just whatever answer feels cool for you. If you've never done this before, treat it like an experiment. You're going to have to play around with different options and combinations of different parts of options to find your best answer.

Regardless of what you choose, notice one theme, though: everything involves you getting back in touch with yourself, through some type of use of words. Expression matters, and your words matter. Use your words. (And I'm saying that to you in my absolute best, most sincere 'mom voice' because I really super-duper-extra mean it!) Speak about the impact of the problems you've faced and the mountains you've climbed in the process of overcoming them.

Your story matters.

EXPRESS THE IMPACT JOURNAL PROMPT

What do you fear when it comes to expressing how you're impacted by the problems you've dealt with? How could your life change by telling your story either more, or at all?

10

RECOVER

'Self-care is giving the world the best of you, instead of what's left of you.'

— KATIE REED

Self-care became all the rage in the mid-2000s, and the intensity people had about it shot quickly to a deafening roar. From yoga studios, to gyms, to nail and hair salons, to massage and bodywork salons, it felt like people just shouted at each other about how *amazing* their self-care was because they went to their 67th hot yoga class of the week, drank celery juice, hit this <*totally rad*> personal record on their deadlift, and, and, and... it just never stopped.

What happened in the process of this, though, was that a really important thing actually became really diluted. Self-care went from being a true act of nurturing, to being this watered-down thing that people did for bragging rights and social points.

When self-care gets diluted, distorted, or whatever you want to label it, it turns from being an act of nurturing to being an act of self-indulgence. Now, self-indulgence from time to time is cool. And when we only engage in it from time to time and keep self-indulgence more limited, there's nothing wrong with it. It feels good, it's exciting, and it gives immediate feedback to our nervous system about fun, happy things. But that's also just the thing: the immediate feedback is really just instant gratification. While it feels great in the moment, the impact of instant gratification is always going to be fleeting, which leaves people chasing more, and more, and more. It feels great in the moment, but it isn't real nurturing. It's important to keep perspective on that and realize the difference in self-indulgence and self-care so that you, me, and all of us can get back to the root of what self-care was always intended to be.

We've got to stop with the bragging rights and get back to the root of self-care, while actually creating real time for true, real self-care to happen. In all seriousness, the cost of not doing so is just too high.

My parents raised me with an incredible work ethic. This is a seriously good thing, and has helped me scale some pretty tough – but rewarding – mountains in my life. However, it's also a not-so-good thing, because I have very little 'chill' in me and love to work. Like I really, *really* love to work. This means that taking time off, going on actual, real-life vacations, spending intentional time with friends, having time to putter around in my garden or crochet something cute (I've got grandma hobbies and I'm *stellar* at making flat things; don't ask me to make a hat – it'll be weird), sit and read a book, or just play with my kid or my dog… it has to be scheduled in or I won't do it. I'll just work instead.

This has been a recipe for burnout quite a few times in my adult life, and it's also led to some gnarly stuff happening in relationships that mattered to me when I didn't prioritize them the way they should have been. It's impacted the way I've felt about myself in the past, and I have spent many years in a state of 'always tired', far too over-caffeinated, and joking that I'd sleep when I was dead. Yes, it's a *terrible* joke.

I showed up to be a worker bee constantly. I was always at work, whether it was my actual job, showing up to help friends or family where they needed it, doing home improvement projects when I was married, or figuring out how to build businesses – it just never stopped. I never took the time to replenish what I gave out to the world, and, because of that, I personally operated at a deficit all the time. I was always exhausted, could catch a cold at the drop of a hat, argued with romantic partners all the time about my work schedule when they wanted me to take time off, and was just all around unavailable for the fun parts of life.

It was no way to live.

Over time, the term 'self-care' started to get irritating to me, not only because it had been so watered-down by different groups, but because it was a constant reminder of a thing I knew I needed and didn't feel I had the time or space to prioritize.

And therein lies the rub.

Most of the time, we're inundated with demands in our lives.

Solve this problem!
Do this thing!
Change that other thing!
Lose that weight!
Remember that thing I said!
Help me with this!

It feels like living each day just to get yelled at over how much faster you have to move, see how many more problems there are still left to solve, what things you need to be responsible for in this moment versus the next and who you have to do those things on behalf of, and more. No wonder we've lost sight of what it means to take actual care of ourselves.

Here's the thing: you can understand all the things about self-care, all the moving parts, all the reasons and explanations and the science behind it, yet none of that matters if you don't make intentional time for it. Today, self-care is a scheduled time block in my calendar every single day. I know this about myself at 41 years old: if I don't schedule it, I'm not going to do it. Plain and simple. It's just too easy to get caught up in the busiest parts of life, and I'm no more or less immune to that than you are. But if it's scheduled, that's a game changer. When I put self-care time into my calendar, regardless of if it's to go exercise, schedule time in with friends, have a planned mommy-daughter date with my kiddo, or just schedule time in to sit on the couch and watch a movie, I do it. It's not negotiable if it's in my calendar.

So what's self-care, anyway?

This is an act of *recovery* and *restoration*. When you practice self-care, especially on the back end of working through a problem, the goal of self-care is to recover from the energy draw of what you just had to do and restore you back to your baseline level of functioning – or better. ('Or better' is definitely better.) As we go through life, deal with all the shit that can get thrown at us, work out the problems we're confronted by, level up, change, and more, there's a sort of 'taking' that happens. Life is great – don't get me wrong – but it takes effort and energy to do life well. In order to continue doing life well, continue to work out problems as they happen, and be an all-around baddie, you're going to have to show up restored, which means self-care becomes a 'have-to' instead of an 'I'll get to it later, I just have to do this other thing first'. So schedule it.

Once you have that time set aside in your calendar, or you've prioritized it in your top three 'to-do's' for the day, then it's on to deciding how you want to use that time. This should be mostly self-care, and a little bit of self-indulgence, because, again, self-indulgence in moderation isn't terrible. It just has to be managed. To stay clear on the differences, let's call self-care 'relief', and let's call self-indulgence 'reward'.

Obviously, the emphasis here is going to be on doing things that leave us with a feeling of relief. That's the main course. The dessert – which is always smaller – is reward. In order to handle doling out healthy percentages of both relief and reward to yourself, I'm a big fan of the 80/20 rule. This says that 80% of the time, you're going to focus on relief and do the things that leave you feeling rested, restored, and ready to go again, because this is where you'll get the most bang for your energetic buck. 20% of the time, you're going to just do fun shit. Being able to choose what you're going to do, based on your needs, does matter here.

In order to get back to the root of what self-care was originally intended to be, I created a system called 'The 5 Bs' for my therapy clients to follow. I was tired of watching good people struggle under the weight of responsibility and problems, forcing themselves to exist dead-freaking-last on their priority list. The 5 Bs was an easy system for them to remember, and using categories made it easier for them to organize their thought process about what they actually needed in order to feel restored. As you go through each of the Bs, I'll give you examples of what self-care and self-indulgence can look like.

The 5 Bs are effective, they're simple, and they're straightforward. But they only work if you make time for them. They are:

Brain
Body
Bonds
Beliefs
Behaviors

Brain

Self-care for your brain is anything you can do that's a thought-provoking activity. Basically, anything that makes you think at a deeper level. Examples include:

- Do a puzzle
- Journal

- Go to therapy
- Read a book
- Work on a craft (one of my best friends personally sews her daughter's entire Halloween costume every year, and her creations are absolutely magical)
- Have a deep conversation with a close friend

You're not limited to these examples – this is just to get you started. If you notice here, these activities all include things like being more mindful, slowing down intentionally, and focusing on connecting more deeply to what you emotionally feel.

Self-indulgence for your brain is anything you can do that lets you veg out, not have to think, or turn into the human version of a potato. Examples include:

- Watch reality TV
- Mindless social media scrolling
- Netflix binging

This isn't about thinking hard, or even thinking at all. It can feel (and be) rewarding to literally check out of reality for a while sometimes, but just remember that this isn't about restoration. This is about indulging.

Body

These are the Big Four that we're told are the only self-care activities we're supposed to do:–

- Exercise
- Eat mostly whole food most of the time

- Drink water (because really, most of us are just dehydrated, overly emotional houseplants)
- Sleep/practice active recovery (the average adult needs 7-9 hours of sleep a night, and you're not just aiming for quantity here – you *also* need to aim for quality. Go down the rabbit hole and look up The National Sleep Foundation, at www.sleepfoundation.org. They're a great resource for starting to learn about sleep hygiene.)

Self-care is all about being as specific as possible with what we're doing and why we're doing it. These four things are the foundational parts of a well-rounded self-care practice, but just be clear on that they're *only* self-care for your body. Once you have a good foundation established for caring for your body, you can add from there.

Self-indulgence for your body are things that make you feel mushy:

- Eating your favorite ice cream
- Going for a massage (this can *also* be self-care if you use bodywork for things like pain management, lupus, or anxiety control, for example)
- Getting your hair done

There are plenty of other things that can be added here – the key is keeping perspective that rewards for our body are usually things that can be stuck into luxury categories. Notice, though, the point about massages/bodywork. There are things and activities that can show up in any category of the 5 Bs that start out as rewards or indulgences, but depending on your reasoning for them, they can turn into relief, restoration, or rest. Most of the time, people get a massage because it feels good and it's relaxing. But if you're diagnosed with lupus, you may require regular massage work as part of your medical care. Knowing the reasoning for choosing a particular activity is what defines it as a relief or as a reward.

Bonds

Before thinking about your bonds – your relationships – we need to hit a hard pause and look at the different kinds of relationships that we don't normally spend time thinking about.

First, let's just acknowledge that social media is a whole thing that's taken over a huge part of our lives. It's a fantastic example of *parasocial relationships*. These relationships happen when you're investing a ton of your time, mental bandwidth, and emotional energy into a person who has zero clue that you even exist. As I write this, Taylor Swift and Travis Kelce of the Kansas City Chiefs are on social media, in the news, and on all things NFL media, with their budding relationship – and the Swifties are absolutely *here for it*. The Swifties – Taylor's loyal followers – are putting all their emotional energy into supporting someone they idolize, while this woman is just getting her groove on, having fun with her new beau, and is entirely unaware of the individual people who make up the Swifties. They're giving her their energy, and getting none of hers back. It's a parasocial relationship.

Then, there's the relationship you have with yourself. This one is the absolute most important relationship you have, and it's typically the one that all of us will prioritize dead flat last. And why? We're taught and told over and over again that our responsibility is to be something, constantly, on behalf of someone or something else. But here's the thing: you can't give yourself to someone or something else if you're not something to yourself *first*. Being something on behalf of the world around you, before you take the time to be something for yourself, is exactly the thing that's going to set you up for failure. This is where the 'operating on a deficit' snowball effect starts. Eventually, that deficit isn't going to just be a snowball anymore – it'll be a whole avalanche that's about to wreck your world. Let's not allow that, shall we?

Finally, there's your moolah. Dolladollas. Dinero. Buckaroos. You know, your *money*. If you're not aware that you have a relationship with your money, bestie,– get aware of it right now. This is typically in the top five of the most impactful relationships any of us can have. While it may be with an inanimate thing, the relationship is just as real, and just as emotional, as any other relationship you could have. If you've ever heard the saying that 'money buys happiness', this is exactly what I mean. This is a relationship that gets all your emotions – good and bad, happy and sad, stressed and chilled – involved. When you have a lot of money in hand and your spending/expenses are well managed, there's a good chance you're going to feel good and at ease. When you don't have that balance, it's easy for money to make you (and me, and any of us) anxious. This is where people, regardless of how much income they actually have coming in, get impulsive, spend on dumb shit they can't truly afford, develop gambling issues, steal, and more. When the total money you have is really close to what your total expenses are, it's crazy-making. It's necessary to take the time to understand what your *money story* is: this is the story of what money represents to you. Is it something that represents all your stress because you feel broke all the time? Or is it something that represents ease because you view money as a tool that facilitates? Talking (and writing) about money stories is another entire book, and there are many, many books already published that take people through this kind of work. If you're not familiar with the idea of money stories, I strongly recommend you get familiar with it, and make sure you get your money story squared away so that you can have a healthy relationship with your cash.

So now that we've established that three important, often-overlooked relationships you have to consider are parasocial relationships, the relationship you have with yourself, and the one you have with your money, let's talk about self-care for our relationships. This is where we need to do things like:

- Establish and maintain reasonable, realistic, and achievable expectations for yourself and others
- Set some boundaries (because you weren't created to be a doormat...)
- Surround yourself with people who lift you up and challenge you to rise to your potential

That last point is the one I want you to really pay attention to when it comes to having relationships with other people. Yes, having solid expectations and setting boundaries are hugely important, but (and I'll die on this hill) the people you choose to surround yourself with are even more important. Our relationships have several metric tons worth of influence in our lives, because of two fun, little nerdy things called *'mirror neurons' and 'mimetic desires'.*

Mirror neurons help drive us to mimic, or copy, other people's behaviors as a way of learning, building understanding, and realizing emotion and intention in ourselves and others. On the other hand, mimetic desires are things we mimic from the people around us because they have something we subconsciously want.

Think of it this way: babies learn how to talk by watching and listening to their parents. When they watch their parents talk, mirror neurons will fire in the baby's brain, and eventually they will start to babble as they try to mimic the gestures their parents make. One day, those mirror neurons will have fired enough, and the baby will slowly start to form actual words and talk. (And then the parents will need to buy stock in quality earplugs, because, holy moly, kids make a lot of noise.)

Pre-teens and teens are a great example of mimetic desire at work – attempts at fitting in really just lead to turning into a copy/paste version of the next kid, and the next kid, and the next. (I mean, who doesn't remember how desperately we all tried to fit in with the cool kids in high school, instead of just being a nerd, or a jock, or a band or choir geek?)

Mirror neurons and mimetic desire are parts of how human nature is hardwired into us. If we know that we're not going to be able to stop ourselves from mimicking the people around us, we have to look at the quality of the relationships we choose to keep.

The higher quality our relationships are, the (generally) better our mental health will end up being, because not only do high quality relationships give us a sense of belonging, but they reduce our tendencies to feel like a burden to the people around us. High quality relationships also hold us more often than not in a place of joy, growth, and having feelings of excitement about the future. When we're surrounded by people who are hard on us really for no reasonable reason, we feel rejected all the time by people we care about. We can end up being constantly told we're not good enough, or we can be dragged into situations that leave us generally feeling crappy. As a whole, these types of relationships just become a drag. It's a drag on happiness, leaving us feeling less connected, more like a burden, and really not thinking about the future at all.

Motivational speaker Jim Rohn said:

> 'You're the average of the five people you spend the most time with.'
>
> — JIM ROHN

And this is absolutely true. Your job, as you practice self-care for your relationships, is to make sure that you're paying attention to the quality of who you surround yourself with so that you become the 'average' you really want. (And don't forget about taking care of the relationships you have with yourself and your money, hunny.)

Now that was a lot of words! Here's some ideas for self-indulgence in your relationships:

- Go clubbing with friends
- Have a pizza and movie night with friends – let it be a PJ party!
- Spend the day at the beach with your partner

Self-indulgence in your relationships is still going to be you spending time with people you care about. The difference here is that you're not doing something to further or deepen the relationship; instead, you're just hanging out and having fun.

Beliefs

The first thing most people normally think about when the word 'beliefs' pops up is religion. That's absolutely part of this, but it's not *all* of this. The word belief means:

1. An acceptance that a statement is true or that something exists
2. Trust, faith, or confidence in someone or something

Beliefs are as much religious views as they are political views, and they're as much your belief in Santa Claus or as much as my daughter believes in the Tooth Fairy. Beliefs run the gamut, but here, we're going to only look at belief in a higher power or something larger than ourselves. When you have a belief in a higher power, whether that's God, Allah, or Yahweh; or Hekate, Lilith, or Odin; or your belief is in something larger than yourself, such as Science – I truly feel there is no 'wrong' belief. There's just what works for you. Having beliefs matters, because this is part of how we figure out what's important to us and what we value. The beliefs any of us can hold also helps us answer hard questions that are normal to ask when we feel like we're suffering, and it helps us assign meaning to things we experience. Here's what self-care for your beliefs can include:

- Go to church weekly
- Set altars based on the Pagan Calendar, or Wheel of the Year
- Do research on topics that interest you about science, the body, emotions, or the environment
- Meet with prayer groups or join a bible study
- Practice rituals, either religious or spiritual
- Join a trail cleanup for your local hiking area
- Volunteer with a forestry team to plant trees or help take care of a state park

On the flip side, self-indulgence for your beliefs could be:

- Buy a fancy rosary you've been eyeing
- Hang a shelf that's dedicated to your crystals
- Scope out a new incense scent from your local supplier, even if you already have enough incense for the next year
- Go walk barefoot in the grass, because you like the way it feels on your feet (just like I mentioned under 'Body' when we talked about massages – walking barefoot in the grass can count as grounding, and it also can be a spiritual practice depending on your beliefs. The perspective you have about an activity or practice is the deciding factor for if it's relief or reward. There's no wrong answer.)

These are still ways you're getting into your beliefs, but they're just focused on fun and being in the moment.

Behaviors

Last but not least! Behaviors are the 'doing' part of both self-care *and* self-indulgence. We can't have the relief or the reward without taking action first, after all. When we look at behaviors as part of self-care and self-indulgence, this is about what we're choosing to focus on from one moment to the next, along with what we're choosing to actively prioritize.

You could have a moment of saying to yourself, 'man, I really want to go work out because I haven't in a couple days, and I know I've got some pent up crap I need to get out. Throwing some weights around would feel really good.' And so off you go to the gym, you exercise for an hour, and leave there feeling happy, energized, and like you've got your head screwed on straight again. Right? In that moment, you chose to prioritize self-care for your body. Totally cool.

But then you get home, and you know that mint chocolate chip ice cream in your fridge is just calling your name. You don't want to deny yourself, but you also don't want to overdo it and mess up progress you're making in the gym by overeating empty (but delicious) calories. So you take your toddler's bowl out of the cabinet so that it automatically forces you to have a smaller serving, fill it up with two scoops of that minty goodness, and off you go to sit and enjoy it. You chose to prioritize self-indulgence for your body in that moment, but you actively moderated it and didn't let it get out of control. Sweet, sweet success.

These two examples are both based on the different self-care and self-indulgent choices you could make for your 'Body'. But notice that the 'Behaviors' you choose are really how the other four categories manifest and show up. 'Behaviors' are the way we express the different categories of self-care and self-indulgence in the process of living well.

Each part of your self-care plan and process matters. One part is not more or less important than the other; your job is to keep in perspective the purpose that each part serves. You don't have to do something from each of the 5 Bs every day either – you just need a plan. You could have a plan to go to church once a week, head to the gym four days a week, and have at least one outing with friends or your girlfriend/boyfriend/partner weekly. You could also plan to journal for ten minutes every night as part of your bedtime routine. Do what works for you, and then be as consistent as possible with it.

Remember, this is all about slowing down intentionally and making time for you to do the things you both want to do and need to do. When you spend all your time trying to bulldoze your way through life, you're eventually going to run out of gas. The more you take time to take care of yourself – especially after you've drained your energy from working out a problem – the more successful you're going to set yourself up to be. And who doesn't like a bit of success, eh?

RECOVER JOURNAL PROMPT

How have you been neglecting your self-care? Or how have you been rocking the self-care game? Have you been doing too much self-indulgence without realizing it? Where do you feel like you could make your self-care practice stronger? What would you like that to include or look like? Why?

A RECAP OF POWER

Pause for Perspective

Addressing a problem effectively is nearly impossible if you're doing it while your nervous system is on fire. Take a moment to actively calm your body and your brain down enough so you can focus and think clearly before proceeding.

Observe and Organize

Take the time to see the forest through the trees (observe) before jumping in to address a problem, or you might miss something important. As you observe the different parts of the problem, sort out which information you need to focus on, and which information is irrelevant (organize).

Work the Problem

Working the problem means taking a problem to the point of either management or complete resolution by: 1) simplifying with specificity (using the information you gathered in

'Observe and Organize'), 2) controlling the controllables, and 3) using a decision tree to streamline your thought process and efforts.

Express the Impact

Talk it out. Expressing the impact a problem has had on you and your life is a relief valve we all need. This can be done through journaling, going to therapy, or talking with a close friend or family member.

Recover

Taking a problem to the point of management or full resolution is exhausting. Take good care of yourself, using 'The 5 Bs' as a system to structure your thought process about self-care.

THIS ISN'T THE END – IT'S JUST THE BEGINNING

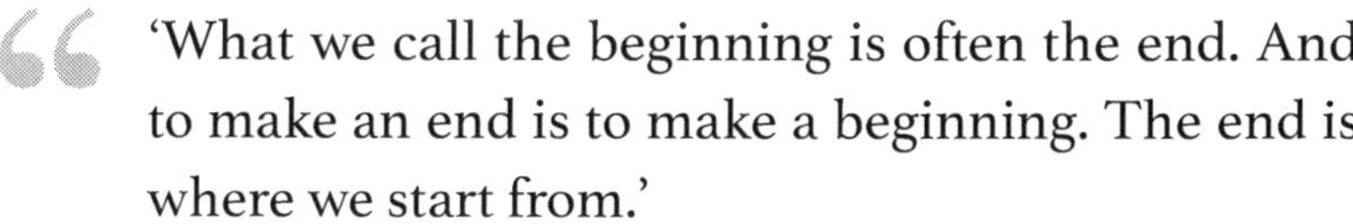

> 'What we call the beginning is often the end. And to make an end is to make a beginning. The end is where we start from.'
>
> — T. S. ELIOT

This is the end of the book – but it's not the end.

This is where you get started, because this is the beginning of you.

This book is jam-packed on purpose, because to stop living according to the past and what you've been told you have to be and start living on your own terms, you need to be able to answer the 'Why', 'What', and 'How' questions I asked you in the introduction:

Why do I feel the way I do/Why am I stuck?
What is it that I don't know?
How can I learn what I don't know?
How do I fix it if it's crappy/How do I enhance it if it's great?

Take a moment here and think about everything you've read, learned, and considered while you were reading about GRIIT and POWER. The answers to those 'Why', 'What', and 'How' questions are on every page of this book, but you have to think critically about them:

1. *Why do I feel the way I do?* – The answer is in every pillar of GRIIT. The act of abandoning yourself for the sake of living on the terms of the world around you will leave you feeling stuck 100% of the time. To change that, go back to the pillars. Look at what parts you're missing, which parts need more attention and to be shored up, and what you need to continue to practice to make the changes and progress you're looking for.
2. *What is it that I don't know?* – The ideas, skills, and behaviors presented in each pillar of GRIIT are meant to either give you new information that deepens your understanding of why mindset and changing your behaviors matter so much, or to remind you of what you already knew. After all, you've always been your own best expert, because no one but you is able to live your life. Use the ideas and skills in GRIIT to remind you of that.
3. *How can I learn what I don't know, and how do I apply it?* – This is the entirety of POWER. There's a saying: 'You

> don't know what you don't know, until you realize you don't know it'. When you're in the process of changing so you can become who you've always been meant to be, you're going to be uncomfortable. The change process highlights insecurities, deficits, fears, and more. Working through those things, in order to apply new information and continue on the path of becoming, means you have to work through the problem-solving process... *a lot.* Use POWER to discover what you don't know, and when you find that information, use POWER to apply it in a way that works best for you.

Without the answers to each of those 'Why', 'What' and 'How' questions, people get lost. This is why the self-help industry is a billion-dollar industry, because gurus have gotten really, really good at turning people into 'forever customers' by holding back on the answers.

You deserve to step out of that customer lineup, and just do you, your own way, on your terms. No more being a prisoner of the past, being tied to everyone else's expectations of you, being a means to an end for the people you're surrounded by, or showing up dead last on your priority list.

That ends *now*, because you just took a seriously deep dive into each of the answers for 'Why', 'What', and 'How'. If you really want what you say you want, now's the time to start proving it to yourself. You have the information you need, you have the strategies, and you have the start of your very own playbook.

Now the work begins.

GRIIT is the way to rework how the past has impacted you, taking with you only the lessons that you need and leaving the rest behind. These pillars are the way to keep yourself from getting lost ever again by constantly reminding you who you are, what you both deserve and choose in life, and why living with audacity, fully on your terms, is the only option from here on out.

POWER is the way to work through the problems that are inevitable for any of us to face – remember, they're speed-bumps, not dead ends. The pillars here serve as a reminder that you are so much more powerful than you think or feel you are. Your power is reflected through taking the time to slow down and really think through different options, so you can solve and manage problems confidently, efficiently, and on your own terms.

A mentor once said to me:

'All that people want to know is the answer to three questions:

Is it possible?

Do I have permission?

> *Will you go with me?*
>
> When they can answer those three questions in the affirmative, that's when they change and start to succeed.'

I was floored in the moment of us talking about this, partly because he essentially summarized my master's degree in all of three sentences, but also because he was entirely correct.

These three incredibly simple questions are also three of the most deep and profound questions any of us could ask. Think about it: if you've ever asked questions like 'are you sure' or 'is this ok' to someone, you're asking about possibility and permission. If you've ever asked for help, you're asking someone to stay with you and be a companion through something.

Any of us – myself included – just want to know that the risk of trying to live well, on our own terms, is really worth it. We want to know that it's ok to go against the grain, and that if we choose to go our own way, we won't have to do it alone.

Let this be the loudest permission slip you've ever had before:

The only way to live well, to live boldly, and to live authentically, is to do it your own way, no matter what anyone else says. Do it your own way according to the playbook and rules you've written solely for yourself, and no matter how many times you fall, get back up – *and quickly.*

Use the chaos, the frustration, the fear, the (fill in the blank with whatever you feel) as your fire, and make it count.

Surround yourself with a bunch of stubborn badasses, who will be the biggest hype crowd you've ever had, and who will happily invite you to be part of their hype crowd. You'll never regret it.

And know, as I said to you when you started this book, when you live rebelliously and with the audacity of someone with unrelenting determination to succeed at being happy on your own terms...

Absolutely anything is possible.

Go live well, do it your way, and as I say to my daughter every day:

Go be great.

If you're looking for more information or ways to work with me, find me at:

Website

www.thegriitproject.com – You can follow the blog, join my email list, find both free and purchasable digital resources, and keep an eye out for webinars and classes.

Social Media

You can find me on Facebook, Instagram, LinkedIn, and YouTube.

Speaking

I can be hired for corporate and wellness trainings, speaking events, and consultations for all things mindset, problem-solving, and self-leadership. Head over to www.thegriitproject.com/speaking for more information.

Individualized Support

If you'd like to become a client, email me at kelly@thegriitproject.com and let's talk. I'm looking forward to it!

Made in the USA
Middletown, DE
08 September 2024